GEORGIA BONESTEEL'S
Bright Ideas
for
LAP QUILTING

Oxmoor House®

**The Leaf Looker
by Georgia Bonesteel**

To quiltmakers
and quilt dreamers:
Let your vision
seek out bright
ideas.

Library of Congress Catalog Number: 90-61776
Hardcover ISBN: 0-8487-1003-7   Softcover ISBN: 08487-1184-X
Manufactured in the United States of America
Second Printing 1993

Executive Editor: Nancy J. Fitzpatrick
Director of Manufacturing: Jerry Higdon
Associate Production Manager: Rick Litton
Art Director: Bob Nance
Copy Chief: Mary Jean Haddin

Bright Ideas for Lap Quilting

Editor: Susan Ramey Wright
Contributing Editor: Charlotte Hagood
Assistant Editor: Virginia A. Welch
Senior Designer: Earl Freedle
Photo Stylist: Katie Stoddard
Assistant Copy Editor: Susan Smith Cheatham
Editorial Assistant: Alice L. Cox
Production Assistant: Theresa L. Beste
Senior Photographer: John O'Hagan
Additional Photography: Gary Clark, Vann Cleveland,
Colleen Duffley, Mary-Gray Hunter, Bruce Roberts
Artists: Samuel L. Baldwin, Larry Hunter

CONTENTS

INSPIRATION

When our foremothers sat down with their hoarded fabric scraps and worn clothing to make warm covers, they had no books or store-bought patterns to help them create their quilts. Instead, they looked to their imaginations. Their patterns reflected the things they saw around them every day: flying geese, turkeys, bears, mountain peaks, ocean waves, starry skies, log walls. Some patterns also came from the pages of the Bible—the only book many families owned. Jacob's Ladder, Crown of Thorns, and Star of Bethlehem are a few.

Bright Ideas for Lap Quilting is meant to stir your creative juices and help you find the inspiration to design your own patchwork. Explore the world around you to find ideas for original quilts, but hold fast to the time-honored quilting traditions that the mothers of our craft invented out of necessity.

The life of today's quilter is often a balancing act between her craft and her everyday activities. But those activities can be much more than a source of irritation. The talented quilter can find bright ideas in even the most mundane corners of her life.

"Sew along with me; the best quilts are yet to be."

One of my favorite folk art sculptures is this piece called The Balancing Act. *It reminds me of the balancing act that today's quilter must perform between her craft and the other interests and responsibilities that claim her time and mental energies.*

Sources Far and Near

Ideas for quilts can come from your imagination or memory, deriving from dreams or past events. Or they can be born of any of thousands of sensory experiences. Stimuli are everywhere—in music, art, nature, advertising, children at play, household pets—anywhere there is something to see or hear or feel.

Some of the best quilt design inspirations could be right under your feet. I incorporated this floor tile pattern into the Masks, Moose, and Qupak *quilt on page 46.*

To record new visual images, take your camera along on vacations and use it liberally. Landscapes and seascapes offer many design possibilities. Explore shops, museums, architecture, and local customs for ideas. These sights can influence style, design, and color, allowing you to grow in your craft.

My teaching experiences on cruise ships gave me the ideas for three of the quilts in this book:

Cruise and Quilt Banner, page 52; *The Big Ship,* page 54; and *Moonbeams Over Many Ports,* page 56. A visit to Alaska gave birth to *Masks, Moose, and Qupak.*

Just like our foremothers, we can find bright ideas for quilts in our own backyards. Houses, shops, sidewalks, flower gardens, autumn leaves—all the everyday sights and sounds in our hometowns can provide material for quilt designs.

Just look out your window. Nature's bounty will inspire you. In reading about the Autumn Windows *quilt on page 22, you'll learn how a box of colorful autumn leaves, sent across the miles from a friend, provided the bright idea for a magnificent quilt.*

What better place to relax and have fun than on a cruise ship! But even when relaxing, keep your quilt brain awake for quilt design possibilities. As you'll see in the "Vacation Quilts" chapter of this book, some of my favorite quilt designs were inspired at sea.

The Geometrics

Beginners often ask me for the easiest patterns. Students entering contests want some tips for winning designs. I always tell them to, "Study the geometrics."

You'll find geometric patterns all around you. Mountains, trees, houses, boats, even animals—all are made up of circles, squares, triangles, and rectangles.

Beautiful landscapes like this Smoky Mountain scene can spark new quilt designs. Mountains, valleys, and celestial bodies are full of geometric patterns. And even a child can find enchantment in clouds.

Shop for Bright Ideas

Never pass up a drafting supply shop or the art and design section of a college bookstore. These stores routinely stock a potpourri of books and supplies with strong design orientation. Designs from such books grew into the bands of colored cloth that dominate the string quilts in the "String Fever" chapter.

Study the designs of other crafts such as stained glass making, needlepoint, and rug hooking to get crossover ideas for your favorite craft. And the ultimate inspiration may be a leisurely visit to the fabric store. Stroll through the aisles of fabric bolts, getting lost in the colors, textures, and designs.

The Truest Form of Originality

Sometimes new quilts emerge from past mistakes. I misplaced a triangle in my first attempt at the *Star Glaze* quilt. So I felt compelled to remake it. This time around I changed the border design and introduced a larger print to make the quilt on page 34.

Perhaps imitation is the sincerest form of flattery, but making a mistake is one of the truest forms of originality.

Stay Open to New Ideas

Don't be afraid to experiment. Gambling with a unique fabric or turning a block sideways can be the "Voila!" or "Eureka!" experience that makes your quilt special.

Quilt blocks need not be cast in stone—as these are. The beautiful Ferguson Fountain at Mars Hill College, Mars Hill, North Carolina, stands eight feet tall and more than 20 feet wide. Its 280 ceramic tiles depict 84 traditional quilt block designs from quilts made by Appalachian Mountain women.

Attitude is a critical part of quiltmaking. Never say never. What you imagined could never happen, just might! To me, compass designs always seemed impossible to re-create in cloth. But with dogged perseverance, I did it! Not once, but twice, in *Golden Threads, Silver Needles I* and *II*.

Keep an open mind for anything and everything new in the way of fabrics, patterns, and techniques. Remember that stretching your mind and attitude is the first step in creating special quilts.

Our quilt well will never run dry as long as we search, think, dream, and desire. There are as many new quilts to be made as there are sets of hands to make them.

Come on, sew along with me; the best quilts are yet to be.

Let your imagination be your mental lighthouse, lighting the way to quilting masterpieces.

When broken down into its simplest parts, basic geometric shapes, a compass design like the ones in the "Warm the Walls" chapter becomes a puzzle in patchwork that is solved as seams join.

HOMETOWN QUILTS

You can wander far and wide, but isn't it a surprise when you find inspiration right outside your own back door?

Bricktown

Bricktown

While I was in Alaska, class member Pam Bickford adapted the herringbone brick pattern to a piecing design. I have used that design in *Bricktown*.

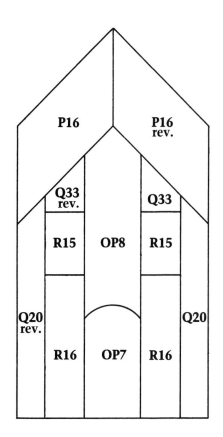

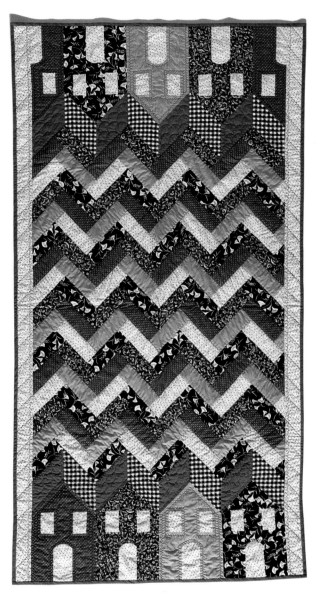

Finished Size: 38" x 72"
Perimeter: 220"
Blocks: 7 (8½" x 17") House blocks
2 (4¼" x 17") Half-house
blocks

Fabric Requirements:

Large black print	¾ yard
White print	2¼ yards
Pink moiré	¾ yard
Dk. blue print	¾ yard
Small black print	¾ yard
Teal	⅜ yard
Black check	⅜ yard
Backing	2¼ yards
Teal for binding	¾ yard

Pieces to Cut:

OP7	9 white print
OP8	2 large black print
	2 pink moiré
	2 dk. blue print
	2 small black print

P16	8 teal
	8 black check*
Q20	4 large black print**
	4 pink moiré**
	4 dk. blue print**
	4 small black print**
Q24	3 large black print
	3 white print
	3 pink moiré
	3 dk. blue print
	3 small black print
Q33	4 large black print**
	4 pink moiré**
	4 dk. blue print**
	4 small black print**
R7	21 large black print
	21 white print

	21 pink moiré
	21 dk. blue print
	21 small black print
R15	16 white print
R16	4 large black print
	4 pink moiré
	4 dk. blue print
	4 small black print
T46	3 large black print
	3 white print
	3 pink moiré
	3 dk. blue print
	3 small black print
2½" x 72½" strip	
	2 white print

*Reverse template.
**Reverse template for half the pieces.

Quilt Construction:

1. Following block diagram on page 11 for placement, make 7 house blocks and 2 half-house blocks. When joining P16 unit (roof) to roof line of house, stitch from side of house to corner dot at roof peak. Backstitch. Break off thread. Insert needle at corner dot on opposite side of seam allowance and stitch to other side of house. To make half-house blocks, mark vertical center lines on OP7 and OP8 templates. Add seam allowance to center edge of each half-template.

2. To make center section, start piecing at bottom edge of Row 1(see Diagram 1). Join strip 1 (large black print Q24) to strip 2 (white print R7). Leave final ½" of seam unstitched as shown in Diagram 2, Figure 1.

Join strip 3 (pink moiré Q24) as shown in Diagram 2, Figure 2, stitching entire length of seam. Join strip 4 (dk. blue R7), leaving final ½" of seam unstitched as shown in Diagram 2, Figure 3. Continue adding strips in same manner, following the 5-color sequence in photograph on page 11.

3. Referring to Diagram 1, piece 4 panels as shown, using Q24 and R7 pieces on Row 1, R7 pieces on Rows 2 and 3, and R7 and T46 pieces on Row 4. (Join T46 triangles to R7 rectangles before completing Row 4.) Leave final ½" of seams unstitched on *both* sides of Rows 2 and 3.

4. Join Rows 1 and 2, beginning at top of panels and working down. (Match edge by using notches in Diagram 1.) Join Row 2 to Row 3 and Row 3 to Row 4 to complete center section.

5. Join house blocks as shown in photograph. Join house rows to top and bottom edges of center section.

6. Join side borders to quilt.

7. Machine-quilt with a feather stitch as shown in photograph. Hand-quilt a scallop design in roof area. Bind with teal fabric.

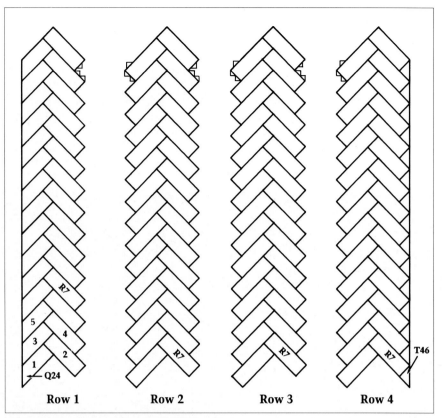

Diagram 1: Assembling and Joining Rows

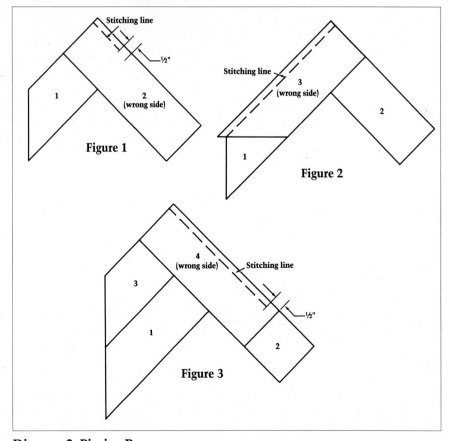

Diagram 2: Piecing Rows

Dewey Decimal 746

The library is a wonderful source of quilting information! Here's a trivia tidbit that all quilters should know. The Dewey decimal number for all quilting books is 746. Check it out—anywhere, in any hometown.

This friendship quilt was made by the Landrum Library Quilters in Landrum, South Carolina, for their retiring librarian, Ruth Farrar. Each book is made from a different calico, and each quilter's name is stitched into her book's spine.

Finished Size: 74" x 84"
Perimeter: 316"
Blocks: 42 (10"-square) Book blocks

Fabric Requirements:

Assorted prints and solids	1¾ yards total
Muslin	3¾ yards
Dk. blue print	1¾ yards
Rose print	2½ yards
Backing	5 yards
Dk. blue print for binding	⅞ yard

Pieces to Cut:

OP12	42 muslin
OP17	42 dk. blue print
P15	84 assorted prints*
R4	42 assorted prints and solids
R5A	84 dark blue print 26 muslin
S1	224 assorted solids
T62	84 dk. blue print*
2½" x 68" strip	2 muslin
2½" x 78" strip	2 muslin
4½" x 77" strip	2 rose print
4½" x 86" strip	2 rose print

*Reverse template for half the pieces.

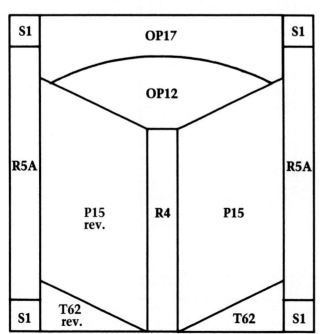

Book Block

Quilt Construction:
1. Following block diagram on page 14 for placement, make 42 blocks as follows: Join OP12 to OP17. Join T62 to P15 (book cover). Repeat with reversed T62 and reversed P15 pieces. Join book cover units to R4 (spine), stopping at top corner dots and backstitching. Join R4 to OP12, backstitching at each corner dot. Sew remaining angles outward on each side of R4. Join 1 S1 to each end of 1 dark blue R5A. Repeat for 1 more S1/R5A unit. Join 1 S1/R5A unit to each side of book block.
2. Set blocks together in 7 rows of 6 blocks across (see quilt diagram below). Join rows.
3. Attach 1 S1 to each end of 1 muslin R5A. Repeat 25 times for a total of 26 units. Join S1/R5A units end to end to form 2 rows of 6 and 2 rows of 7. Attach 1 (6-unit) row to top and 1 to bottom of quilt top. Join 1 remaining S1 piece to each end of each 7-unit row. Join 1 (7-unit) row to each side of quilt top.
4. Join 2½"-wide muslin inner borders to sides of quilt, mitering corners.
5. Join 4½"-wide rose print outer borders to sides of quilt, mitering corners.
6. Quilt as desired. Bind with dark blue print fabric.

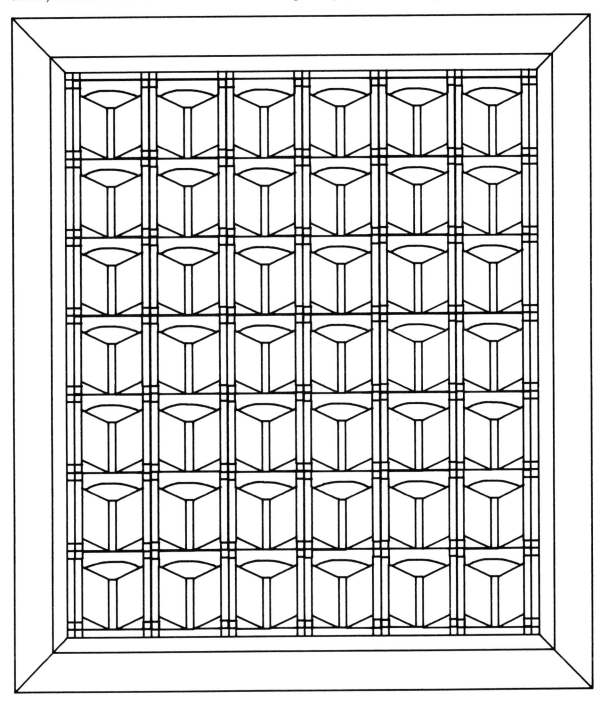

Bed of Roses

Soft and sweet as an Indiana rosebud is this group quilt. The blocks are set on point to contrast with quilted muslin blocks. Many hands came together from the Quilters' Guild in Bloomington, Indiana, to stitch this magnificent raffle quilt. But it took just one hand to pull the winning ticket from the hat—mine!

Finished Size: 84" x 105"
Perimeter: 378"
Blocks: 20 (10⅝"-square) Rose blocks
         30 (6" x 12") Rosebud Border blocks

Fabric Requirements:

Dk. green	1½ yards
Dk. rose print	¼ yard
Med. rose print	5½ yards
Lt. rose print	⅝ yard
Muslin	6½ yards
Green print	2⅝ yards
Backing	6 yards
Dk. rose print for binding	⅞ yard

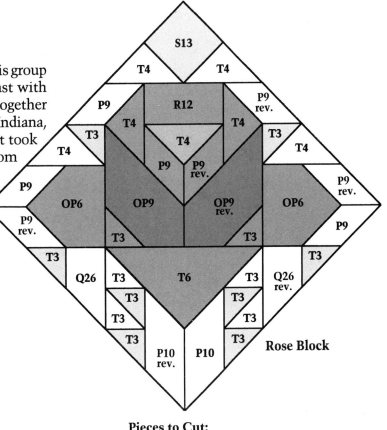

Rose Block

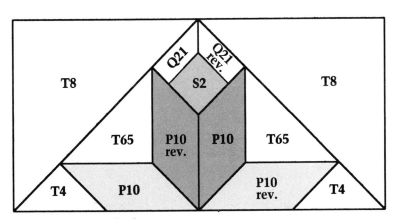

Rosebud Border Block

Pieces to Cut:

OP6	40 med. rose print
OP9	40 lt. rose print*
P9	40 med. rose print*
	120 muslin*
P10	40 muslin*
	60 med. rose print*
	60 dk. green*
Q21	60 muslin*
Q26	40 muslin*
R12	20 med. rose print
S2	30 dk. rose print
S13	20 dk. green
T3	160 dk. green
	80 muslin
	40 med. rose print
T4	140 muslin
	40 med. rose print
	20 dk. rose print
T6	20 med. rose print
T8	60 muslin
T65	60 muslin
11⅛" square**	12 muslin
11⅝" square**	7 muslin
11⅞" square**	1 muslin
6½" x 10½" rectangle	2 muslin
4½" x 6½" rectangle	2 muslin
1½" x 6½" strip	2 muslin

*Reverse template for half the pieces.
**Cut edge of square on bias.

Quilt Construction:

1. Following block diagrams on page 17, make 20 rose blocks and 30 rosebud border blocks. Set aside.

2. Cut each of the 7 (11⅝") muslin squares in half diagonally to make 14 side triangles. Cut the 11⅞" muslin square into quarters diagonally to make 4 corner triangles.

3. Following quilt diagram below, set together rose blocks with 11⅛" muslin squares and side and corner triangles.

4. Following quilt diagram, join 5 rosebud border blocks to form bottom border. Cut 1 (2½" x 60½") strip from green print and join to bottom of unit. Cut 2 (2½" x 60½") strips from rose print and join to top and bottom of unit. Join border unit to bottom of quilt top. Cut 2 (2½" x 87½") strips from rose print and join to the sides of the quilt.

5. Join 7 rosebud border blocks to form right border. Join 1 (1½" x 6½") muslin strip to bottom edge of unit (see quilt diagram). Cut 1 (2½" x 85½") strip from green print and join to right edge of unit. Cut 1 (2½" x 8½") strip from rose print and join to bottom edge of unit. Repeat for left border, except join green print strip to left edge of unit. Join side borders to sides of quilt top.

6. For top border, make 1 row of 5 rosebud border blocks and 1 row of 6 rosebud border blocks. Join 1 (6½" x 10½") rectangle to each end of the 5-block row. Join 1 (4½" x 6½") rectangle to each end of the 6-block row. Join the 2 rows as shown in diagram. Cut 1 (2½" x 80½") strip from green print and join to bottom of unit. Cut 2 (2½" x 80½") rose print strips and join to top and bottom of unit. Join border unit to top of quilt top.

7. Follow quilt diagram to cut 2 (2½" x 105½") medium rose print strips and join to sides of quilt.

8. Quilt as desired. Bind with dark rose print fabric.

Spotlight Dancing Spools

Quilter Thelma Caldwell sent me a roughly sketched graph for a Dancing Spools quilt. She requested that someone who knows about ballet improve it. For me, this meant a trip to the library to rediscover the dance positions. Each spool ballerina wears a net tutu and illustrates a different ballet stance. Appliquéd toe shoes and quilted legs accent the panel at center top.

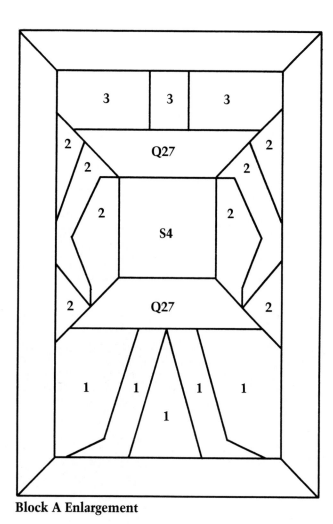

Block A Enlargement

Finished Size: 34" x 56"
Perimeter: 180"
Blocks: 10 Ballerina blocks
       1 appliquéd panel

Fabric Requirements:

Muslin	1¾ yards
Dk. blue	1¾ yards
Pink	½ yard
Pink net	¼ yard
Assorted scraps	⅓ yard
Backing	1¾ yards
Dk. blue for binding	⅝ yard
Pink satin ribbon (¼"-wide)	1 yard

Pieces to Cut*:

Q27	20 assorted
R1	2 muslin
S1	2 muslin
S4	10 assorted
T63	6 red
4½" x 30¾" strip	2 dk. blue
3¾" x 73½" strip	1 dk. blue
1¼" x 8½" strip	10 pink net

*Refer to Step 1 to make templates for remaining pieces.

Quilt Construction:

1. Enlarge gridded blocks on page 125 onto gridded freezer paper. (Enlarge asymmetrical blocks C, H, and I onto shiny side of freezer paper.) Code templates in order of piecing (see Block A Enlargement). Color each numbered group of pieces a different color.

2. To cut and make blocks, refer to Gridded Freezer Paper as a Creative Tool, page 120. Gather net strips and baste to tops and sides of tutus. Appliqué shoes and ribbon ties onto rectangle at top center of quilt.

3. Refer to quilt diagram and photograph on page 21 to set blocks together with 1" mitered borders and solid rectangles to form 2 horizontal rows. Join horizontal rows.

4. Piece step sections and join to lower edges of side border strips. Join top, bottom, and side borders to quilt.

5. Hem 1 long edge of each 4½" x 30¾" side curtain strip. Gather all ends to a width of 3". Hem ends and 1 long edge of 3¾" x 73½" top curtain strip. Gather long raw edge to a width of 48½". With raw edges aligned and hemmed edges toward center, baste top and side curtains to outside edges of quilt borders (see photograph).

6. Stack backing, right side down; batting; and top, right side up. Quilt outlines of ballerinas' legs (see photograph and gridded pattern). Other quilting lines represent spotlight rays, radiating upward from behind each ballerina. Note seats and audience quilted on bottom border. Bind with dark blue fabric.

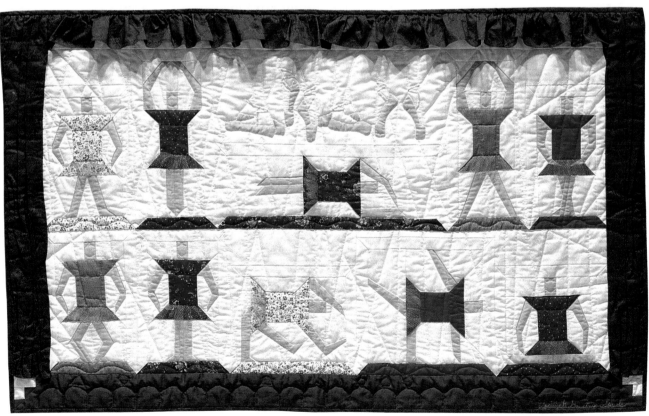

Autumn Windows

Now you can save the vibrant colors of autumn leaves in cloth. Maple leaves from Maine became Alice Thomure's inspiration for this unusual quilt. Leaves are simply photocopied, transferred to freezer paper, and then cut from richly hued fabric. Appliqué the branches and leaves against white windows to suggest colorful fall foliage dancing in the crisp autumn air.

Alice chose to cross-hatch the solid squares in a double line of quilting, with straight lines behind the leaves. (The photograph below shows the bottom half of the quilt only.)

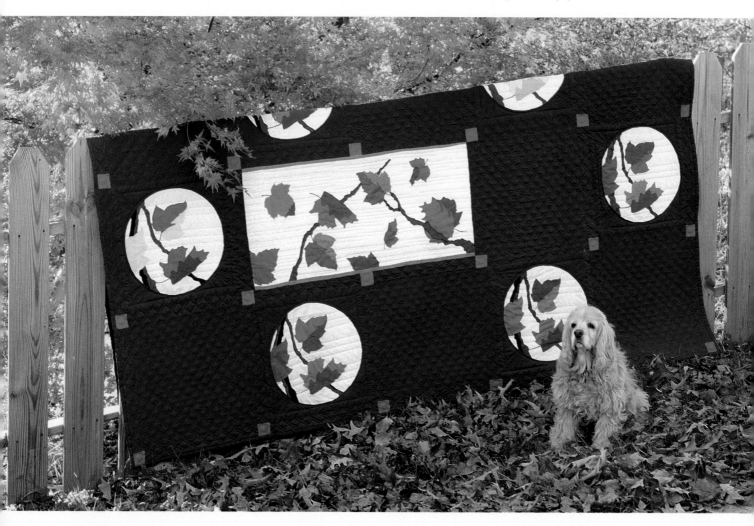

Finished Size: 102" x 102"
Perimeter: 408"
Blocks: 10 (18"-square) blocks with
    circles
    11 (18"-square) plain blocks
    2 (18" x 38") rectangles with
    ½" x 38" accent strips

Fabric Requirements:

Navy	8½ yards
White	3⅞ yards
Red	½ yard
Brown	1 yard
Assorted scraps in autumn colors	2 yards total
Backing	9⅜ yards
Navy for binding	1 yard

Pieces to Cut*:

18½" square	21 navy
2½" x 18½" strip	58 navy
17½"-diameter circle	10 white
19½" x 40½" rectangle	2 white
1" x 38½" strip	4 red
2½" square	36 red

*Refer to Steps 1–2 to cut remaining pieces.

Quilt Construction:

1. Photocopy selected leaves to make templates for leaf appliqués. Trace templates onto dull side of freezer paper and cut out. Iron templates to right side of leaf fabrics and cut out, adding ½" seam allowance to each piece.

2. Cut lengths of brown fabric in desired shapes and sizes to represent tree limbs (see photograph).

3. Position leaf and limb appliqués on white circles and rectangles (see photograph). Stitch close to freezer paper around leaves and close to raw edge on limbs. Peel off freezer paper. Trim fabric as close to stitching line as possible.

4. Place a piece of lightweight paper under white fabric and outline each leaf and limb with narrow zigzag stitch, covering previous stitching line. Adjust width of zigzag stitch so that it narrows at leaf points. To stitch inside curves, lower needle into fabric on inside of stitching line, raise presser foot, pivot fabric, lower presser foot, and gently guide fabric as you stitch around curve. On outside curves, lower needle on outside of stitching line and proceed as above. Satin-stitch leaf stems as shown in photograph. Peel paper from behind fabric.

5. To reduce bulk in appliqués, trim away white fabric underneath each appliqué, leaving ¼" seam allowance all around.

6. Adding appliqués could cause the fabric to draw up a bit, and the cutting dimensions I have given allow for this. After adding appliqués, trim circles to measure 15½" in diameter and rectangles to measure 17½" x 38½". Join red accent strips to long edges of rectangles. Turn under seam allowances and hand-appliqué circles to navy squares. To reduce bulk, trim away navy fabric under circles, leaving ¼" seam allowance.

7. Join red accent squares to sashing strips to make horizontal rows of sashing (see quilt diagram). Following quilt diagram, set blocks and rectangles together with sashing.

8. Quilt as desired. Bind with navy fabric.

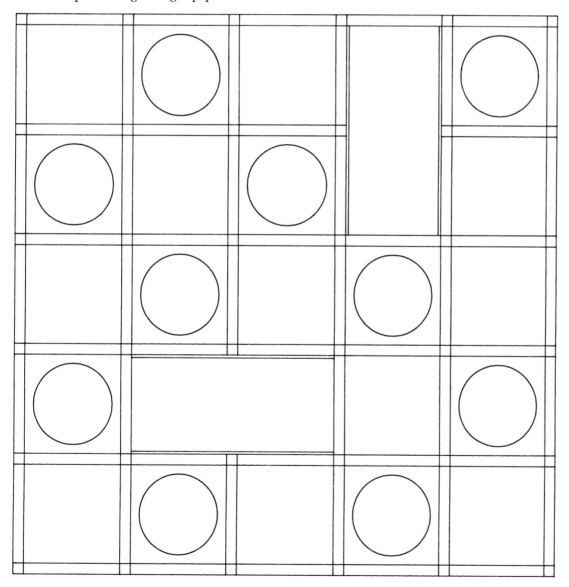

Little Toot

Inspired by a colorful toy box, Marilyn Fluharty brightened her grandson's room with this train quilt. Three rows of trains, coming and going, span the top. Picture strip piecing, based on a grid and sewn with freezer paper strips, helps this project move along into the station quickly. Cut fabric in duplicate with your rotary cutter in fast-forward motion!

Finished Size: 60" x 105"
Perimeter: 330"
Blocks: 12 (12"-square) Car blocks
3 (12"-square) Engine blocks

Fabric Requirements:

Blue	2 yards
Red	1¾ yards
Green	1¾ yards
Yellow	¼ yard
White	2 yards
Ticking	1¾ yards
Backing	6½ yards
Red for binding	⅞ yard

Pieces to Cut*:

10½" x 60½" strip	1 blue
15½" x 60½" strip	1 blue, 1 red, 1 green
2½" x 60½" strip	3 ticking
4½" x 60½" strip	1 ticking, 1 blue

*Refer to Step 2 to cut remaining pieces.

Quilt Construction:

1. Enlarge patterns on page 129 onto shiny sides of 2 (12") squares of gridded freezer paper.
2. Refer to Picture Strip Piecing, page 120, to cut and make blocks, following block diagrams below to join pieces. Refer to photograph for color placement, or place colors as desired.
3. Set blocks together in 3 rows as shown in quilt diagram.
4. Complete quilt top by joining train rows with colored strips of fabric as indicated in quilt diagram and photograph. Appliqué wheels to train cars as shown in diagrams.
5. Quilt as desired. Bind with red fabric.

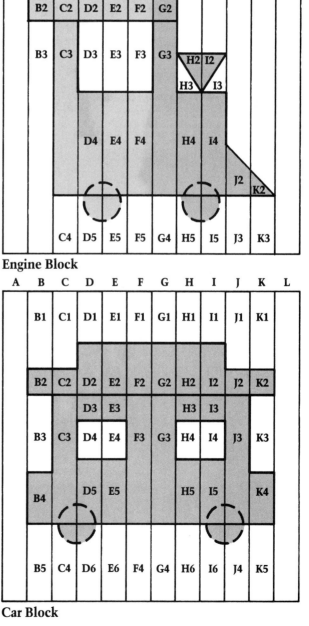

Engine Block

Car Block

Hillside Village

The twenty houses in this quilt illustrate how using both the right and wrong sides of fabric can create a play of light and shadow. The side of the roof (template T1) and the side of the house (template P5) are cut from the reverse side of the fabric.

This design may look familiar to you. Its little sister, a 36-inch x 46-inch Hillside Village wall hanging, has already starred in my pattern club, *Spinning Spools*. For the full-sized quilt, I have increased the size of the block from 6 inches to 12 inches, added a window, and designed a new border.

Finished Size: 72" x 92"
Perimeter: 328"
Blocks: 20 (12"-square) blocks

Fabric Requirements:

Assorted prints for houses	1¾ yards total
White print	2½ yards
Assorted black prints	1 yard total
Lt. lavender print	4½ yards
Dk. lavender print	¾ yard
Dk. green print	1¼ yards
Backing	5¼ yards
Dk. green print for binding	⅞ yard

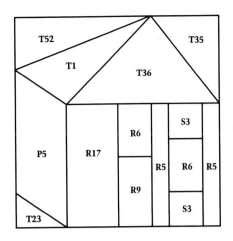

Pieces to Cut:

P5	20 house print */**
Q1	4 black print
R5	40 house print
R6	20 house print
	20 white print
R9	20 white print
R17	20 house print
S3	40 house print
T1	20 black print */**
T19	37 white print
	37 dk. lavender print
	78 dk. green print
T23	20 lt. lavender print*
T35	20 lt. lavender print*
T36	20 black print*
T52	20 lt. lavender print*
2½" x 12½" rectangle	
	2 lt. lavender print
4½" x 12½" rectangle	
	5 lt. lavender print
6½" x 12½" rectangle	
	2 lt. lavender print
8½" x 12½" rectangle	
	5 lt. lavender print
12½" square	3 lt. lavender print
12½" x 16½" rectangle	
	3 lt. lavender print
1½" x 64" inner border strip	
	2 lt. lavender print
1½" x 84" inner border strip	
	2 lt. lavender print
1½" x 66" inner border strip	
	2 white print
1½" x 86" inner border strip	
	2 white print

*Reverse template for half the pieces.
**Cut from reverse side of fabric.

Quilt Construction:

1. Following block diagram (left) for placement, make 10 house blocks. Make 10 more house blocks, reversing order of pieces to make mirror images (see quilt diagram below).

2. Following quilt diagram, set blocks together with background pieces.

3. Add inner borders to quilt top, mitering corners (see photograph and quilt diagram).

4. To make top and bottom outer borders, join dark green, dark lavender, and white T19 border triangles, following quilt diagram and photograph for placement. Follow same procedure for 2 side borders, adding black corner Q1 pieces to ends. Join to quilt top.

5. Quilt as desired. Bind with dark green print fabric.

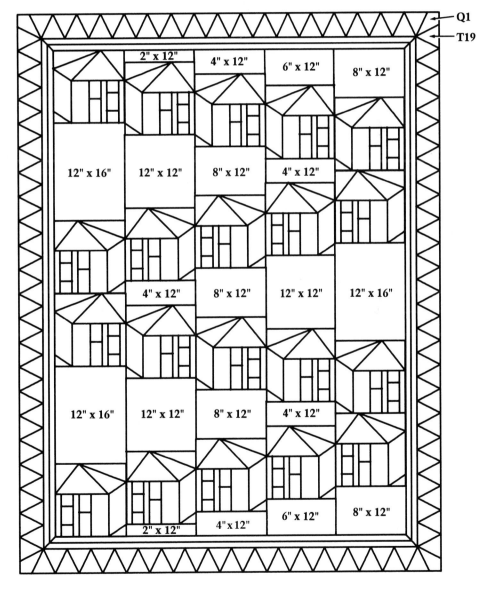

GEOMETRIC GEMS

The following quilts were derived from popular and time-honored geometric shapes—but with a fresh approach.

*Grandma Evans's
Chicken Feet*

Grandma Evans's Chicken Feet

Penny Wortman is a faithful contributor to the lap-quilting field. This scrap medley quilt, which Penny made from her Grandma Evans's leftovers, was lap-quilted. She added the Flying Geese border in sections to the perimeter blocks to be quilted along with the blocks.

Finished Size: 88" x 88"
Perimeter: 352"
Blocks: 25 (16"-square) blocks

Fabric Requirements:

Muslin	6⅛ yards
Assorted pastel print scraps	6⅛ yards
Backing	8 yards
Muslin for binding	⅞ yard

Pieces to Cut:

P8	32 print*
P14	400 print*
R9	100 muslin
S1	16 muslin
S3	100 muslin
T10	16 muslin
T15	300 print
	360 muslin
T46	320 print
8½" square	25 muslin

*Reverse template for half the pieces.

Quilt Construction:

1. Follow large block diagram to piece block as follows: Join 3 print T15 triangles. Repeat for 3 more T15 units. Attach 1 T15 unit to each side of center square and set aside.

Join 2 P14s and 2 reversed P14s to make corner stars. Repeat for 3 more corner stars. Set 2 muslin T15 triangles in each corner star as shown in diagram. Set 1 S3 corner square into each corner star unit. Join corner star units with 4 R9s. Join corner stars to center unit.

2. Using T46 and muslin T15 pieces, piece Flying Geese borders in 8-goose sections. (Note that geese change directions at center of each border strip.)
3. Following small block diagram, piece 4 corner blocks.
4. Following quilt diagram, join Flying Geese border sections and small corner blocks to perimeter blocks. Lap-quilt, using light green quilting thread. Join blocks to form rows. (See Lap-Quilting Connections, page 121.) Join rows. Bind with muslin.

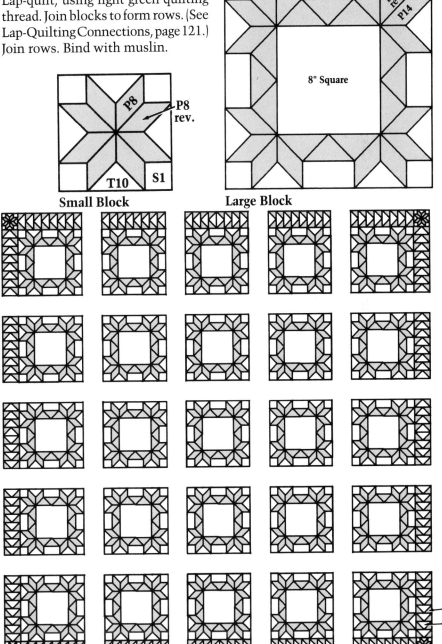

Small Block   Large Block

Plaid Pinwheels

This quilt proves that plaids and checks *can* work in quilts. So don't be afraid to experiment. The simple, straightforward Pinwheel pattern makes this a great quilt on which to use a system of continuous machine-piecing.

Finished Size: 63" x 77"
Perimeter: 280"
Blocks: 99 (7"-square) Pinwheel
blocks

Fabric Requirements:
Assorted plaids
   and checks   5⅛ yards total
Muslin   2 yards
Backing   4½ yards
Muslin for binding   ¾ yard

Pieces to Cut:
Q14   396 assorted plaids and checks
T32   396 muslin

Quilt Construction:
1. Following quilt block diagram, piece 99 Pinwheel blocks as follows: Join T32 to Q14, aligning right angles of each piece.
2. Keep sewing in a continuous chain until 4 sets of matching checks and plaids are linked. Do not cut thread between pieces, but sew "on air" for a few stitches between pieces to create a "kite-tail" of triangles. Clip sections apart.
3. Align 2 matching triangles and join to form a larger triangle. Continue to join matching triangles in a continuous chain without cutting thread as in Step 2. Cut triangles apart, align matching triangles, and stitch to form square. As you sew, press seams in a clockwise direction around block.
4. Join blocks in 11 rows of 9 blocks each. Join rows.
5. Quilt with straight lines. Bind with muslin.

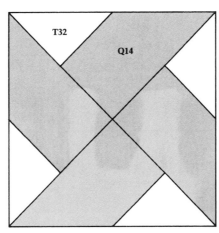

Pinwheel Block

Star Glaze

A bold and beautiful print lends a new look to a classic Virginia Reel setting that, like *Ocean Blue* on page 38, uses the Monkey Wrench block. Try your hand at this tried-and-true block, which is made mostly of triangles surrounding a simple four-patch.

VACATION QUILTS

Keep those design juices flowing—even when relaxing on vacation. New ideas are around every bend in the road.

Masks, Moose, and Qupak

Masks, Moose, and Qupak

The opportunity to travel in Alaska, teaching and taping for the PBS-TV *Lap Quilting* series, has left an indelible impression on me. This quilt, based on my Alaskan experiences, depicts the masks I discovered at the University of Alaska in Fairbanks, the moose I saw minutes after my plane landed, and the qupak technique I learned from Etta Lord.

(Qupak is a decorative trim once made from calf skin and attached to the edges of parkas. Today, single-fold bias tape replaces the calf skin.)

The three Alaskan motifs come together in this strip quilt. Print fabric found in, of all places, the Caribbean islands adds festive flair and charm to the patchwork.

Finished Size: 82" x 102"
Perimeter: 368"
Blocks: 4 (8"-square) Mask blocks
2 (10"-square) Mask blocks
1 (14"-square) Mask block

Fabric Requirements:

Assorted prints	5 yards total
White	2½ yards
Burgundy	2½ yards
Gold	⅛ yard
Backing	6¼ yards
Print for binding	⅞ yard

Pieces to Cut:
8" Mask Blocks

OP26	8 white
OP26A	4 white
OP26B	12 white
OP28	16 print
OP28A	12 print
S3	8 white
S5	4 print
T71	8 contrasting print

10" Mask Blocks

OP2	8 print
OP2A	4 print
OP3	8 white
OP3A	2 white
P18	4 gold
S4	8 white
S15	2 print

14" Mask Block

OP27	8 white
OP27A	1 white
OP27B	1 white
OP29	10 print
OP29A	1 print
P19	2 gold
S16	1 print

Totem Bodies

P2	16 print*
P17	18 print
Q9	13 print
Q11	66 print
S18	20 white
T33	40 print
	4 burgundy
T48	26 white*
T52	32 white
T64	132 white
T66	36 burgundy
5" x 10½" rectangle	2 white
2½" x 8½" rectangle	2 white
4½" x 14½" rectangle	1 white
4½" x 8½" rectangle	4 print
8½" x 14½" rectangle	1 print

Borders

Moose appliqué	5 burgundy
	5 white

*Reverse template for half the pieces.

8½" x 82½" strip	1 burgundy
	1 white
3½" x 82½" strip	1 print
5½" x 82½" strip	1 white
3½" x 78½" strip	2 print
5½" x 78½" strip	2 white

Quilt Construction:

1. Following mask block diagrams, make 2 (8"), 2 (10"), and 1 (14") mask blocks. Machine-appliqué eyes in place. Add purchased rickrack for mouths and beads and buttons for noses and earrings (see photograph).

2. Follow quilt diagram on page 48 to make totem bodies and join them to their respective mask blocks. Join totem bodies, following quilt diagram, to complete totem unit.

3. Attach 1 (3½" x 78½") print strip to opposite sides of totem unit.

4. Following quilt diagram, appliqué 5 white moose to 8½" x 82½" burgundy strip; appliqué 5 burgundy moose to 8½" x 82½" white strip. Join moose strips. Join moose unit to bottom of totem unit.

5. Join 3½" x 82½" print strip to bottom of moose unit.

6. See Qupak Border Construction on page 49 to make 2 (4½" x 78½") and 1 (4½" x 82½") qupak borders.

7. Following quilt diagram, join qupak borders to sides and bottom of quilt.

8. Stack backing, right side down; high-loft batting; and top, right side up. Baste. Hand-quilt around masks and moose as in photograph. Using transparent thread, quilt in-the-ditch along the long vertical seams. (Before machine-quilting, roll the quilt tightly and secure with bicycle clips.

Unroll as you quilt.) Following the photograph, add tie-tacking as final accent, attaching 1 tiny bead to each tie and securing with a double square knot. Bind with print fabric.

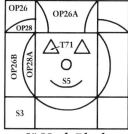

8" Mask Block

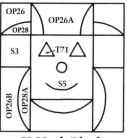

8" Mask Block

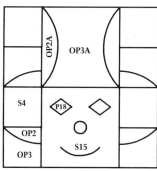

10" Mask Block

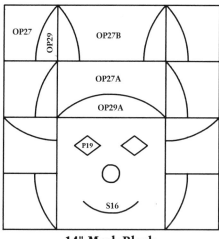

14" Mask Block

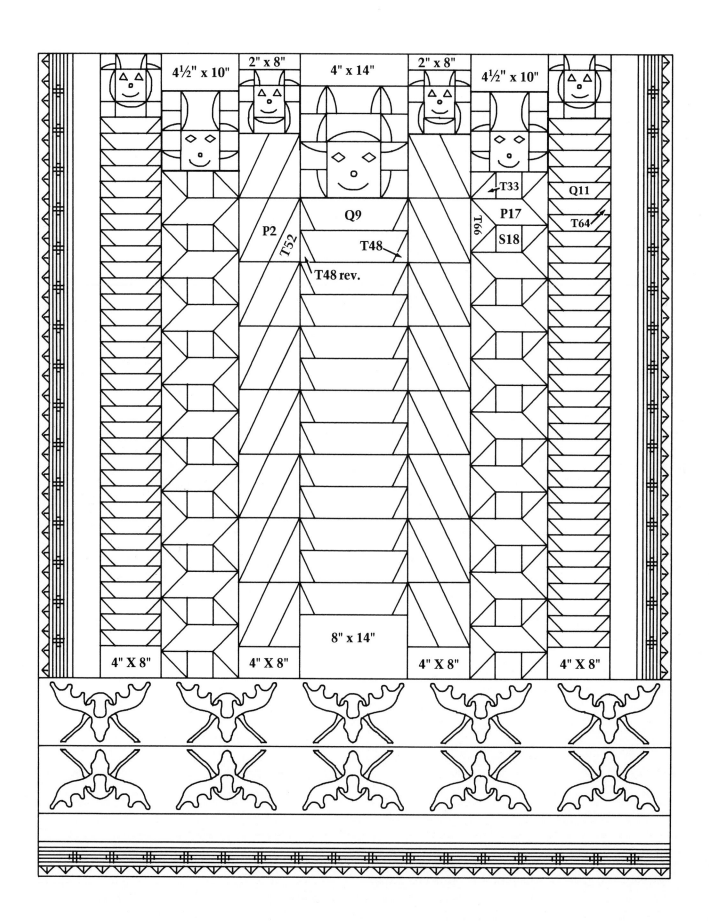

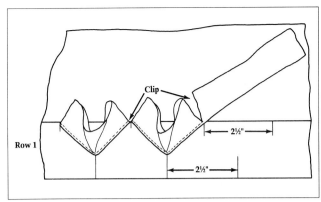

Diagram 1

Qupak Border Construction:

1. To make qupak borders, you will need the following amounts of single-fold bias tape (either purchased or handmade) in colors of your choice: 16½ yards (1"-wide) for Row 1 "rickrack" edging; 6¾ yards (⅞"-wide) each for Rows 2-6; and 5½ yards (½"-wide) for cross strips.

2. To make bottom border, use 5½" x 82½" white strip for foundation fabric. (Use 5½" x 78½" white strips to make side borders.) Mark straight lines across foundation 2" from outside edge of border, 1" apart, as sewing guide. Also mark midpoints, 2½" apart, between these lines (see Diagram 1). This will be the placement line for "rickrack" edging.

3. For Row 1, refer to Diagram 1. To make points of "rickrack" trim, with 1"-wide bias tape (plaid "rickrack" in photograph), position tape as shown and edgestitch point-to-point. With needle down at placement line, clip bias tape on top edges as shown in diagram to release fabric to make next point. Continue in same manner, placing points an equal distance apart across width of foundation fabric (see quilt diagram and photograph).

4. Using ⅞"-wide bias tape, position bottom edge of tape so that it just overlaps top edge of "rickrack." Fold tucks in "rickrack" points in same direction (see Diagram 2). Edgestitch bottom edge of tape in place to complete Row 2.

5. Using another color of ⅞"-wide bias tape, position this strip across top edge of first strip ½" above stitching line for first strip for Row 3. To make cross strips, insert 1"-long (½"-wide) bias strips of contrasting color under tape between points and stitch (see Diagram 3). See photograph and quilt diagram for placement of these cross strips.

6. Complete Row 4 in same manner as Row 3. As you sew, flip back each cross strip from previous row and insert 1 new cross strip on each side (see Diagram 4).

7. Complete Row 5 in same manner as Row 3. As you sew, flip back each pair of cross strips from previous row and insert another cross strip in between, opposite the cross strip on Row 2 (see Diagram 5).

8. Complete Row 6, flipping back each cross strip from previous row. Edgestitch top of Row 6 bias strip to foundation fabric. (See Diagram 6 for finished qupak border.)

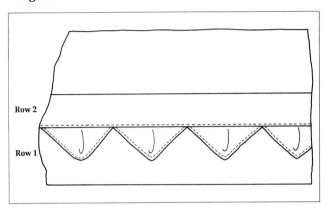

Diagram 2

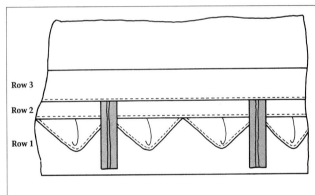

Diagram 3

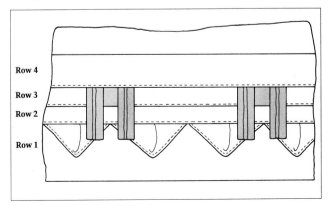

Diagram 4

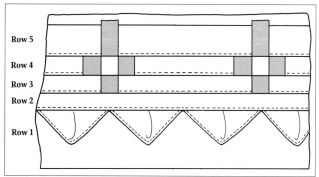

Row 5
Row 4
Row 3
Row 2
Row 1

Diagram 5

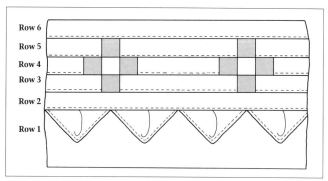

Row 6
Row 5
Row 4
Row 3
Row 2
Row 1

Diagram 6

Qupak Workshirt

The qupak technique is great for adding accents to smaller projects such as totes, vests, and skirts. Here, I've used it to embellish a chambray workshirt.

Material Requirements:

Chambray workshirt with 2 breast pockets

5⅝ yards (1"-wide) single-fold lavender bias tape

1⅜ yards (1"-wide) single-fold turquoise bias tape

1⅞ yards (½"-wide) single-fold navy bias tape

3 yards (1"-wide) single-fold white bias tape

Shirt Construction:

1. Using seam ripper, carefully remove pockets from shirt and set aside.

2. Trim 2" from bottom of shirt. Reserve trimmed fabric.

3. Using seam ripper, carefully separate shoulder seams of shirt.

4. Cut lavender tape into 8 (17½") strips for shirt front, 8 (6") strips for pockets, and 2 (6") strips for bottom front of shirt. Cut turquoise tape into 2 (17½") strips for shirt front and 2 (6") strips for pockets. Cut navy tape into 64 (1") pieces. Cut white tape into 2 (17½") strips for shirt front, 2 (28") strips for "rickrack" on shirt front, and 2 (8") strips for "rickrack" on pockets.

5. See Qupak Border Construction, page 49, to sew qupak trim on front of shirt and pockets, using the shirt as foundation fabric. Place "rickrack" points 1½" from edges of shirt. Substitute bias tape measurements in Step 3 above for measurements in Qupak Border Construction. Add Row 7 of 17½" white bias strips to complete qupak trim.

6. Join shoulder seams.

7. Edgestitch 2 (6") lavender bias tape strips across bottom front of shirt on each side, covering ends of qupak trim and turning under raw edges at ends of tape.

8. Turn under bottom of shirt 1½" from cut edge and press. Turn under a narrow hem along cut edge and press to form drawstring casing. Edgestitch in place.

9. Edgestitch pockets in place on sleeves as shown in photograph.

10. Using reserved fabric, cut and piece a drawstring ½" wide and 36" longer than length around bottom of shirt. Insert drawstring in casing.

Cruise and Quilt Banner

This wall hanging was designed on gridded freezer paper so that the drawn lines become the outlines of the templates. Feel free to add a new star, change the angle of the sun, or spell the name of your ship using the nautical alphabet. The flags here spell the name of the ship that sailed us on a memorable quilting cruise—*Caribe*.

Finished Size: 27" x 32"
Perimeter: 118"
Blocks: 1 (24" x 27") ship panel
      1 (8" x 27") fish panel

Fabric Requirements:

Navy print	⅝ yard
White	¼ yard
Med. blue print	⅞ yard
Yellow print	⅛ yard
Red print	⅛ yard
Green print	¼ yard
Rose print	¼ yard
Multicolor print	¼ yard
Backing	1 yard
Assorted scraps from above fabrics for binding	½ yard total

Pieces to Cut*:

Q17 (with notch)	4 multicolor print
Q17 (without notch)	6 rose print
	6 green print
	2 multicolor print
T39	4 rose print
	4 green print
T54	18 med. blue print

*Refer to Step 3 to make templates for remaining pieces.

Quilt Construction:
1. Following quilt diagram at right, make fish panel.
2. To make fish noses that extend from quilt, with right sides facing and raw edges aligned, sew 2 green print T39 pieces together, leaving 1 end open as shown on pattern. Trim seam, turn, and press. Repeat with 2 rose print T39 pieces. With raw edges aligned, sew green print nose to green print fish on right edge of fish panel; sew rose print nose to rose print fish on left edge of fish panel.
3. Enlarge ship panel pattern on page 127 onto the shiny side of a 24" x 27" piece of gridded freezer paper. (Join lengths of freezer paper to get the correct width by overlapping edges and pressing with warm iron.)

4. Refer to Picture Strip Piecing, page 120, to code freezer paper templates, cut pieces, join strips, and make panel. Refer to photograph for color placement. (*Note:* Pieces outlined with broken lines are to be cut and appliquéd to the finished panel.)
5. Join ship panel to fish panel.
6. Quilt as desired. Piece bias strips of print fabric as shown in photograph and bind edges of quilt. Press extended fish noses toward edge of quilt and tack to binding. Make and attach a casing to back of banner for hanging.

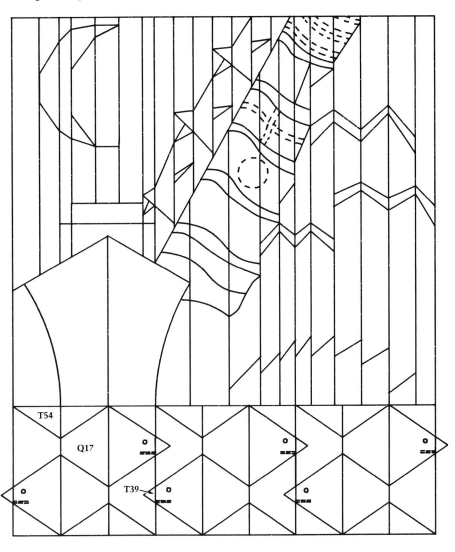

The Big Ship

This quilt is a patchwork souvenir of one of my quilting cruises.

Finished Size: 60" x 60"
Perimeter: 240"
Blocks: 1 (6"-square) Split Star block
4 (12"-square) Sail blocks

Fabric Requirements*:

White	1⅜ yards
Multicolor print	½ yard
Aqua	1½ yards
Yellow	1½ yards
Pink	1½ yards
Backing	3½ yards
Scraps from above fabrics for binding	¾ yard total

*Yardage for pieced sails not included.

Pieces to Cut**:

Q16	4 yellow
S10	1 multicolor print
T20	4 pink
T21	4 aqua
T34	8 white***
12½" square	7 white
	2 multicolor print
12⅞" square	3 white
	1 multicolor print
6½" square	4 white
	4 multicolor print

**Cutting instructions for pieced sails not included. See Step 6 for instructions for cutting wavy borders.

***Reverse template for half the pieces.

Quilt Construction:

1. Cut 12⅞" squares in half diagonally to make 6 white triangles and 2 multicolor print triangles. Set aside.
2. Create 4 sails to fit 1 diagonal half of a 12⅞" square. (If you prefer, cut sails from print fabric.) Join sails to 4 white triangles to make 4 sail blocks.
3. Following block diagram above, piece Split Star.
4. On 1 white 6½" square, measure 4¾" in from 1 corner along raw edge

and mark. Measure 4¾" in from same corner on adjacent side. With straightedge, draw line connecting these 2 points. Cut off corner along drawn line and discard. Repeat with 3 remaining white squares. Follow quilt diagram at bottom of page to

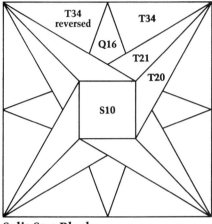

Split Star Block

join these 4 pieces to Split Star block.
5. Follow quilt diagram and photograph to set all blocks and triangles together.
6. To create wavy border, refer to Making Curved Templates, page 120, and make 4 (6½" x 48½") pieced border strips, referring to quilt diagram and photograph for suggested shapes and color placement.
7. Join a border to top and bottom of quilt. Join 6½" multicolor print squares to ends of remaining borders. Join borders to sides of quilt.
8. Quilt letters N, S, E, and W around compass points (see photograph). Radiating lines from sun sail are quilted with metallic thread. The students' names are stitched on waves underneath ship. Piece bias strips of fabric as shown in photograph and bind edges of quilt.

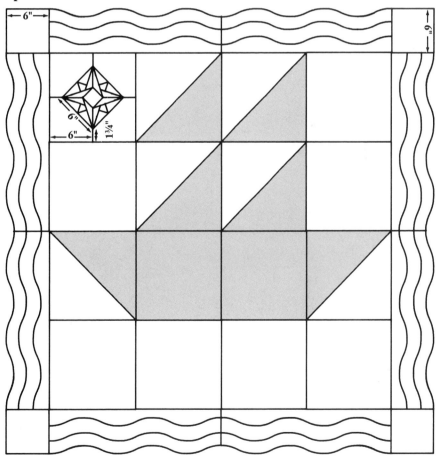

Moonbeams Over Many Ports

A quilter on vacation has a special mission while scouting tourist shops—finding fabric, of course. It's a universal search and the inspiration for many a new quilt. My special background fabric used in this quilt was a real find on Grand Cayman. It is complete with the British flag, pirates, fish, and a map of the island.

Finished Size: 65½" x 78½"
Perimeter: 288"
Blocks: 8 (12"-square) Cruisin' blocks
        8 (12"-square) Moonbeam blocks
        15 (4½"-square) Mini-Cruisin' blocks

Fabric Requirements:

Assorted blue print	3 yards total
Black	1 yard
White	1 yard
Red	¾ yard
Yellow	Scrap
Green	¾ yard
Vacation print	2 yards
Backing	4½ yards
Black for binding	¾ yard

Pieces to Cut*:

OP10	16	vacation print**
OP30	8	black
OP30 reversed	8	white
OP31	16	blue print**
Q3	8	white
Q3 reversed	8	black
Q4	16	blue print**
Q5	30	blue print**
Q7	8	green
	8	red
Q8	8	green
	8	red
Q12	30	blue print**
Q32	15	black
Q32 reversed	15	white
Q34	8	white
Q34 reversed	8	black
R2	8	white
R3	16	blue print
R10	8	red
R11	16	blue print
R14	30	blue print
S1	14	red
	1	yellow
T11	8	black
	8	white
1½" x 28½" strip	8	green
	8	red
1½" x 16½" strip	4	green
	4	red
5" x 26½" rectangle	10	vacation print
5" x 14½" rectangle	4	vacation print

*Refer to Steps 1-2 to cut remaining pieces.

**Reverse template for half the pieces.

Quilt Construction:

1. Enlarge Moonbeams pattern on page 126 onto shiny side of a 12" square of gridded freezer paper.

2. Refer to Gridded Freezer Paper as a Creative Tool, page 120, to code freezer paper templates, cut pieces for moonbeams, and assemble 8 blocks. Refer to photograph for color placement.

3. Follow block diagrams at right to make 8 Cruisin' blocks and 15 Mini-Cruisin' blocks. Join 1 Moonbeam block to top of each Cruisin' block.

4. Follow quilt diagram below to join red and green border strips to sides and top of Cruisin' blocks, mitering corners (see photograph). Add bases to bottom of Cruisin' blocks (pieces T11, Q7, Q8, and OP10).

5. Join Cruisin' blocks to make 4 vertical rows of 2 blocks each. Join 1 (5" x 14½") rectangle to top of each vertical row.

6. Join Mini-Cruisin' blocks to 5" x 26½" rectangles as shown in quilt diagram to make 5 vertical strips. Join vertical strips to vertical Cruisin' rows.

7. Follow print in border for quilting lines and outline-quilt ship and moonbeams. Quilt 1 of the 8 phases of moon in each Moonbeam block (see quilt diagram). Bind with black fabric.

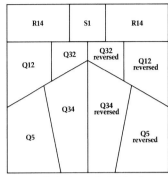

Mini-Cruisin' Block

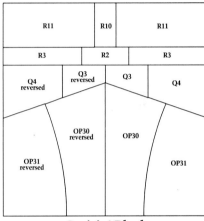

Cruisin' Block

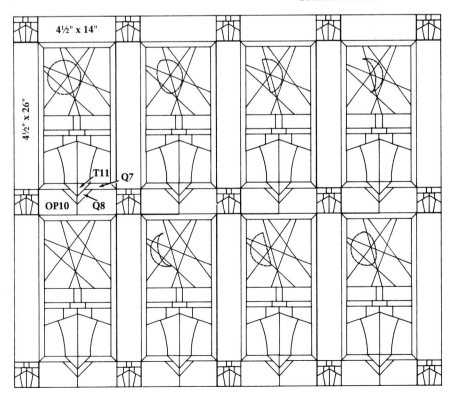

UK Sampler

Years ago, I saw an old chintz quilt in the Victoria and Albert Museum in London. I was amazed to see the feather design appliquéd rather than used as a quilting pattern. That technique is the feature accent on this special quilted tribute to Great Britain.

My quilt begins with a center block of hexagons, whipstitched using English piecing and displaying the letters *UK* for United Kingdom. The sampler blocks have special significance. The Rails blocks represent the British rail system, linking one picturesque city to another. Quilters in England are joined by a guild, and the Guild block is taken from their logo. Finally, the British flag adorns the four outside corners.

The chintz panels were appliquéd with the feather design. I chose to mix various shades of red and blue to match the colors in the British flag.

Finished Size: 90" x 100"
Perimeter: 380"
Blocks: 4 (10"-square) Rails blocks
        4 (12"-square) Guild blocks
        4 (15" x 20") UK Flag blocks
        1 (16"-square) Center UK block

Fabric Requirements:

Flowered chintz	6½ yards
Assorted shades of blue	2 yards
Assorted shades of red	2 yards
Backing	9 yards
Flowered chintz for binding	⅞ yard

Pieces to Cut:
Center UK Block

OP11	45 chintz*
	23 chintz**
Q6	8 chintz*
T16	14 chintz*
T55	4 chintz*

Rails Blocks

P12	8 light red
	8 light blue
	8 dark red
	8 dark blue
Q13	32 chintz
R20	4 light red
	4 light blue
	4 dark red
	4 dark blue
T14	32 chintz

Guild Blocks

Q18	32 chintz
S17	2 blue
	2 red
T63	56 blue
	56 red
	144 chintz
T65	16 chintz

UK Flag Blocks

OP18	16 red/chintz (see Step 12)
R18	4 dark red
R19	8 dark red
T26	16 dark blue
T27	16 dark blue
1½" x 11½" strip	16 chintz
1¼" x 11½" strip	16 dark red
¾" x 11½" strip	16 chintz
⅞" x 9⅛" strip	16 chintz
⅞" x 6⅞" strip	16 chintz

Feather Panels

OP13 (center and end feathers)	
	8 blue
	8 red
OP13	60 blue
	60 red
12½" x 36½" rectangle	
	4 chintz
OP14 (center and end feathers)	
	12 blue
	4 red
OP14	40 blue
	48 red
10½" x 16½" rectangle	
	4 chintz

OP15 (center and end feathers)	
	8 blue
	8 red
OP15	84 blue
	84 red
15½" x 60½" rectangle	
	2 chintz
20½" x 60½" rectangle	
	2 chintz

*Cut from dark area of chintz.
**Cut from light area of chintz.

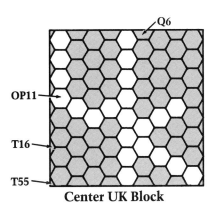
Center UK Block

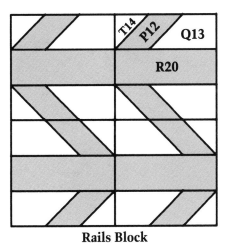
Rails Block

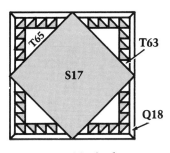
Guild Block

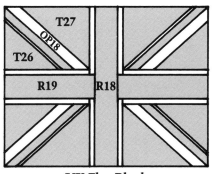
UK Flag Block

Quilt Construction:
1. Read Quilt-and-Extend Method, page 122, before beginning.
2. Referring to Center UK block diagram at left, make UK block, following this quick version of the traditional English hand-piecing method. Transfer finished-size templates (without seam allowance) to dull side of gridded freezer paper as follows: OP11, 68 times; Q6, 8 times; T16, 14 times; and T55, 4 times. Cut out freezer paper templates and center and iron to wrong side of their respective fabric pieces. Finger-press seam allowances to wrong side.
3. With right sides facing and straight edges aligned, match and whipstitch edges to join hexagons, following Center UK block diagram for placement. Fill in edges with Q6, T55, and T16 pieces. Remove freezer paper. Finished block will measure 16½" x 16¹¹⁄₁₆".
4. Cut 1 (16½") square each from batting and backing. Stack backing, right side down; batting; and center block, right side up, easing the 16¹¹⁄₁₆" edges of block to fit the 16½"-square backing. Lap-quilt as desired.
5. Make 4 (10½" x 16½") appliquéd feather panels, using OP14 feathers, as follows: Following quilt diagram on page 60 and photograph on page 61 for placement, trace center line of feather unit on each 10½" x 16½" chintz rectangle to guide placement of appliquéd feathers.

Cut finished-size OP14 template from thin cardboard. Place template on wrong side of fabric piece. Apply spray starch to seam allowances, fold seam allowances over edge of cardboard, and press. Remove cardboard. Place appliqués along traced line and appliqué with lightweight thread, using a running stitch. (See Appliqué Accents, page 121.) Set 2 feather panels aside.

6. Cut 2 backings and 2 battings to match feather panels. Add panels to Center UK block, using quilt-and-extend method.

7. Make 4 Rails blocks, following block diagram on page 59 and quilt photograph on page 61 for placement. Join blocks to ends of 2 remaining feather panels. Cut 2 backings and 2 battings to match units. Layer units with batting and backing. Join these 2 units to sides of center unit as shown in quilt diagram. Quilt.

8. Follow Step 5 to appliqué OP13 feathers to 4 (12½" x 36½") chintz rectangles. Join 2 feather panels to top and bottom edges of center unit as shown in quilt diagram. Lap-quilt as desired.

9. Following block diagram on page 59 and quilt photograph on page 61 for placement, make 4 Guild blocks. Join Guild blocks to ends of remaining (12½" x 36½") feather panels.

10. Follow Step 5 to appliqué OP15 feathers to 20½" x 60½" and 15½" x 60½" chintz panels. Set 20½" x 60½" feather panels aside. Join other 2 feather panels to the long edges of 2 Guild block units as shown in quilt diagram. Join panels to center section and quilt.

11. To make template for quilting pattern on Guild block, fold an 8½"

square of gridded freezer paper in half diagonally. Fold diagonally again and then again, to divide paper into 8 sections.

Transfer the UK quilting pattern on page 127 to folded freezer paper. Cut out design along traced lines through all layers. Unfold, iron to the center of Guild block, and trace around design.

12. To make UK Flag blocks, join 1 (1½" x 11½") chintz strip, 1 (1¼" x 11½") red strip, and 1 (¾" x 11½") chintz strip as shown in the photo-graph to make a striped band. Repeat for 3 more bands. Cut 8 OP18 pieces from striped band; reverse template and cut 8 more. Following UK Flag block diagram on page 59 for placement, join 1 T26 and 1 T27 to each OP18 unit.

Following UK Flag block diagram, join 1 (⅞" x 9⅛") strip to 1 long edge of each pieced rectangle. Join 1 (⅞" x 6⅞") strip to 1 short edge of each pieced rectangle. Join 1 pieced rectangle to each long edge of 1 R19 piece. Repeat with remaining R19 piece.

Join units to long edges of R18 piece to complete flag. Repeat Step 12, 3 times for 4 flag blocks.

13. Join UK Flag blocks to ends of remaining feather panels. Join panels to top and bottom of quilt. Quilt panels. Bind with chintz fabric.

> ### *Bright Idea!*
> *To develop a unique signature touch, try the UK quilting pattern technique (see Step 11) with your own initials.*

Singapore Stars

The teaching location was Singapore; the subject was patchwork stars. Hence the name for a stunning array of star patterns, made by Penny Wortman.

Finished Size: 44½" x 44½"
Perimeter: 178"
Blocks: 4 (10"-square) star blocks
       4 (4⅝"-square) star blocks

Fabric Requirements:

Turquoise	1½ yards
Lt. rose	½ yard
Dk. rose	1 yard
Blue print	¾ yard
Small black print	1⅛ yards
Large black print	⅞ yard
Solid white	1 yard
White print	⅛ yard
Backing	1⅓ yards
Black for binding	¾ yard

Pieces to Cut:
Center Star and Pieced Border

P1	16 turquoise	
	25 lt. rose	
	44 blue print	
	43 small black print	
	35 dk. rose	
	25 large black print	
T32	1 lt. rose	
	1 dk. rose	
	1 blue print	
	1 large black print	

Star and Cross Block

OP1	4 dk. rose
Q22	8 small black print*
S4	4 solid white
S9	4 dk. rose
	4 turquoise
	1 lt. rose
T5	4 solid white

Rising Star Block

P13	4 turquoise**
	4 dk. rose
S4	4 solid white
S12	4 white print
T5	4 solid white
T32	8 large black print
T45	4 white print

Morning Star Block

S14	4 solid white
T42	4 turquoise
	4 dk. rose
	4 large black print
	4 small black print
T65	4 solid white

Grandma's Star Block

S8	1 dk. rose
T14	4 turquoise
T18	4 solid white
T33	4 solid white
	4 white print
T62	4 large black print*
	4 small black print*

Ohio Star Block

S7	4 solid white
	1 large black print
T2	4 solid white
	8 small black print
	4 turquoise
T13	2 solid white
T33	1 solid white

Blazing Star Block

T13	2 solid white
T22	8 solid white*
T33	1 solid white
T56	4 small black print**
	4 turquoise
T61	4 blue print*
	4 dk. rose*

Sawtooth Star Block

S9	4 solid white
T13	2 solid white
T33	1 solid white
T44	8 solid white
	8 small black print
	4 dk. rose
	4 blue print

Another Star Block

S6	1 turquoise
S7	4 solid white
T2	4 solid white
	8 small black print
	4 dk. rose
T13	2 solid white
T33	1 solid white
T43	4 dk. rose

Solid Borders

2¼" x 39½" strip	4 turquoise	
2¼" x 46½" strip	4 turquoise	

*Reverse template for half the pieces.
**Reverse template.

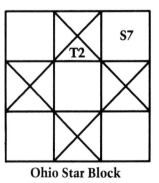

Ohio Star Block

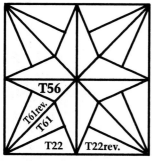

Blazing Star Block

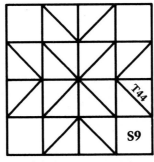

Sawtooth Star Block

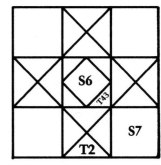

Another Star Block

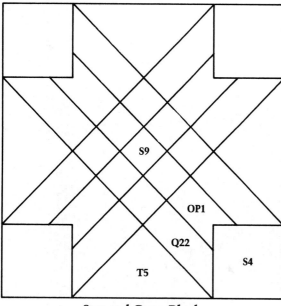

Star and Cross Block

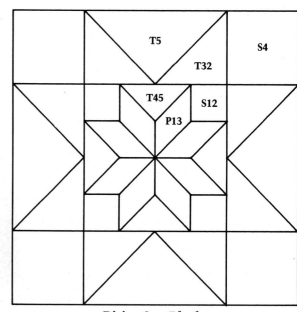

Rising Star Block

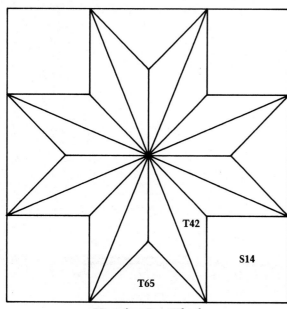

Morning Star Block

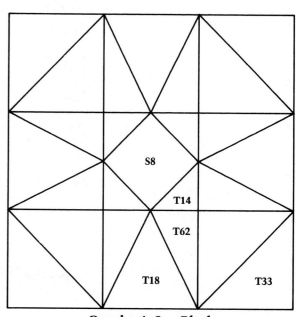

Grandma's Star Block

Quilt Construction:

1. Follow block diagrams and quilt photograph on pages 62–64 to make the 8 star blocks. Complete small blocks by joining T13 and T33 triangles as shown in quilt diagram. Set aside.

2. Follow quilt diagram at right and quilt photograph to make center star.

3. Follow quilt diagram to join star blocks to center star.

4. Follow quilt diagram and quilt photograph to make inner border and to join all borders to quilt, mitering corners.

5. Quilt as desired. Bind with black fabric.

Bright Idea!

The key to success in piecing all acute-angle patterns, such as diamonds or hard-to-sew inside right angles, is to stop at the corner dot and lock the seam in place by backstitching, allowing for a free-floating seam. Lift needle, break off thread, and insert needle at corner dot on other side of seam allowance.

Amish Images

Drive slowly into the world of the Amish and experience their gentle ways and peaceful existence. The bright red and gold patches that form the hazard signs on the backs of their somber buggies provide lasting images—and great quilt inspiration!

Finished Size: 77½" x 102"
Perimeter: 359"
Blocks: 18 (11" x 16") Horse and Buggy
blocks
2 (11" x 13½") appliquéd word
blocks
60 hazard sign triangles

Fabric Requirements:

Assorted red and gold	5 yards total
Black print	4 yards
Gold print	3⅞ yards
Backing	6 yards
Black print for binding	⅞ yard

Pieces to Cut:

OP4*	18 gold print
OP5	18 black print
OP16*	18 black print**
P3*	18 gold print
P4*	18 black print **
P11*	18 black print **
Q19	180 assorted red and gold
T24	50 black print
T25	60 assorted red and gold
T28*	18 gold print
T29*	18 gold print
T40	18 assorted red and gold
	50 black print
T47*	20 black print
T50*	20 black print
1½" x 16½" strip	18 gold print
3" x 9" rectangle	18 gold print
8" x 10½" rectangle	18 gold print
11½" x 14" rectangle	2 gold print
"Amish" appliqué	1 black print
"Images" appliqué	1 black print

*Reverse template for half the pieces.
**Cut pieces from reverse side of fabric.

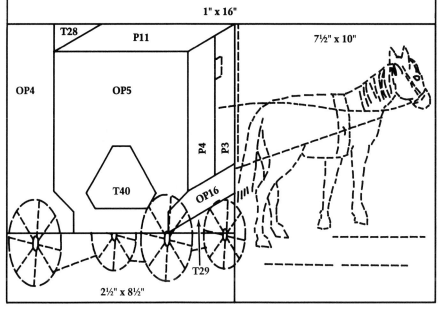

Quilt Construction:

1. Referring to quilt diagram, assemble 10 horizontal rows of hazard signs as follows: Join narrow borders (Q19) to large triangles (T25) to form 60 hazard signs. Join T24 triangles to left edges of 50 hazard signs as shown. Join black T40 triangles to right edges of signs as shown. Join these units in 10 horizontal rows of 5 each. Join 1 remaining hazard sign to left edge of each horizontal row. Join 1 black T47 to right edge and 1 reversed T47 to left edge of each horizontal row (see quilt diagram). Join 1 black T50 to right edge and 1 reversed T50 to left edge of each horizontal row (see quilt diagram). Join horizontal rows as shown in quilt diagram, balancing red and gold colors.

2. Enlarge "Amish" and "Images" word appliqués on page 124. Enlarge Horse and Buggy pattern on page 125.

3. Following block diagram on page 67, piece 18 Horse and Buggy blocks. (*Note:* 9 buggies face in 1 direction, 9 in the other.) Clip corners from the 18 red and gold T40 triangles. Appliqué to backs of buggies. Transfer quilting lines for horse and wheels to right sides of blocks with black indelible pen.

4. Referring to quilt diagram on page 69 for placement, appliqué words to 11½" x 14" rectangles. Set aside.

5. To make borders, join Horse and Buggy blocks and appliquéd word blocks as shown in quilt diagram. Join borders to quilt top.

6. Outline-quilt along lines drawn on Horse and Buggy blocks (see detail photograph above). Outline-quilt around all buggy pieces. Quilt around words in the appliquéd word blocks. Quilt a large A (for Amish) inside each hazard sign T25 triangle. Quilt a triangle inside each black T24 triangle.

7. Bind with black print fabric.

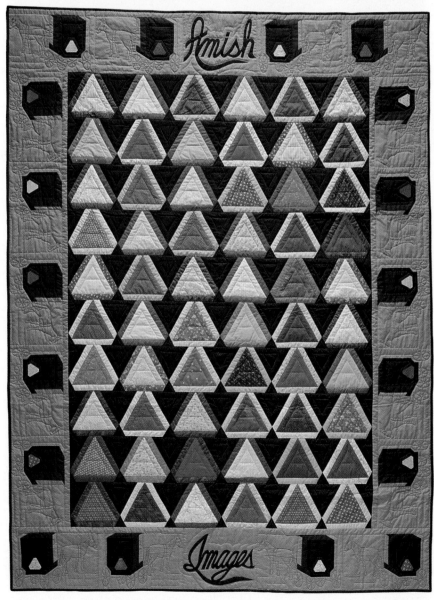

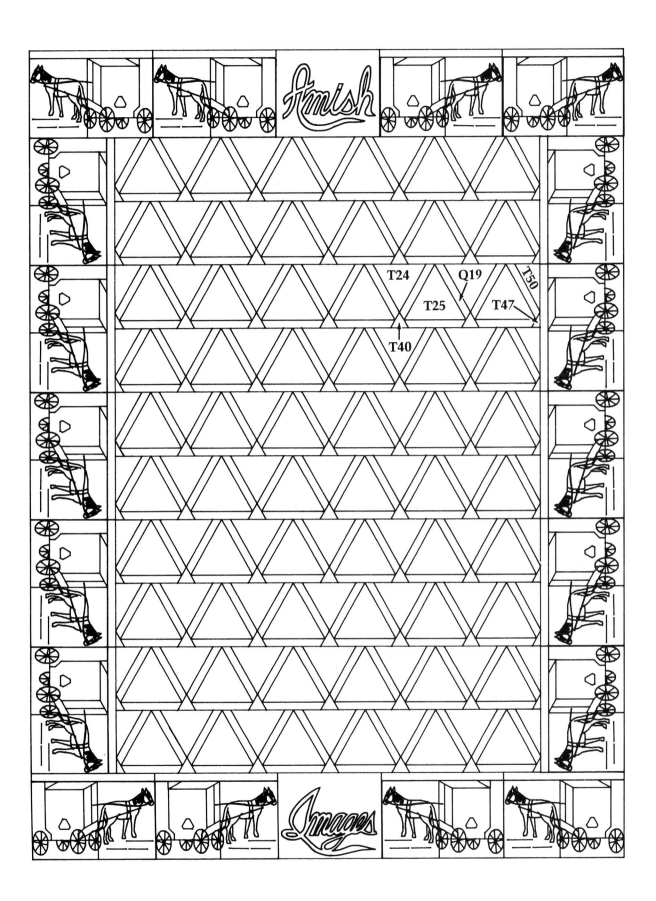

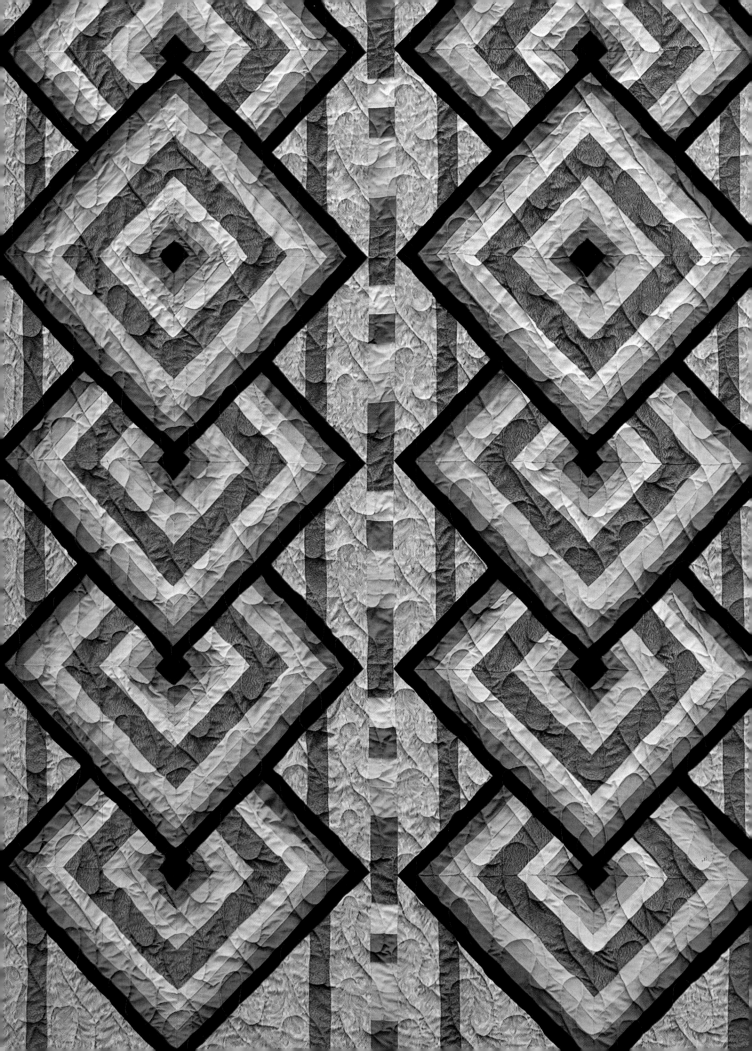

STRING FEVER

Regular bands, exact measurements, and a rotary cutter help update these variations of the old-time string quilt.

Hipp Strip

Hipp Strip

Graduated shades of coral and aqua give this quilt a southwestern look.

Finished Size: 113" x 119"
Perimeter: 464"
Blocks: 64 (14⅛"-square) blocks

Fabric Requirements:

Paisley print	3⅜ yards
Purple print	2½ yards
Black	3 yards
Dk. aqua	1½ yards
Med. aqua	1½ yards
Lt. aqua	1½ yards
Dk. coral	1½ yards
Med. coral	1½ yards
Lt. coral	1½ yards
Backing	10 yards
Paisley print for binding	1 yard

Pieces to Cut:

A*	32	pieced coral-to-aqua stripe
	32	pieced aqua-to-coral stripe
B*	24	pieced coral-to-aqua stripe
	24	pieced aqua-to-coral stripe
Q37	48	purple print
Q38	48	paisley print
Q39	16	paisley print
Q40	16	purple print
T69	48	paisley print
T70	16	paisley print

*See Steps 1–4.

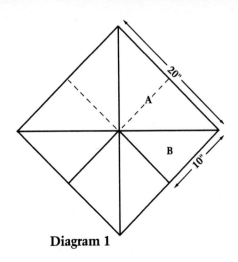

Diagram 1

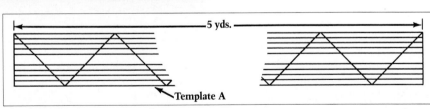

Diagram 2

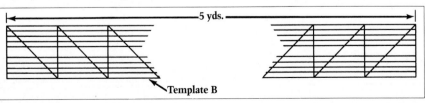

Diagram 3

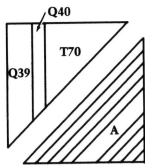

Diagram 4

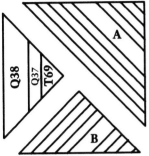

Diagram 5

Quilt Construction:

1. Make templates A and B by folding a 20" square of paper as shown in Diagram 1. Open square. Cut out templates A and B. Redraw templates, adding ¼" seam allowance all around.

2. Cut 20 (1½"-wide) bias strips each from 3 shades of coral, 3 shades of aqua, and black fabrics. Cut 20 (2½"-wide) bias strips from purple print fabric. Join ends of strips with diagonal seams to make 6 (5-yard-long) strips of purple print and of each shade of coral and aqua. Make 12 (5-yard-long) strips of black.

3. Join long edges of bias strips in order shown in photograph (black, dk. coral, med. coral, lt. coral, purple print, lt. aqua, med. aqua, dk. aqua, black) to make a 9-color striped band. Repeat to make 5 more bands.

4. Place base of template A on black and cut 32 striped triangles, shading from coral at outside to aqua at center point, and 32 shading from aqua at outside to coral at center point. (See Diagram 2 for triangle

placement.) Place base of template B on black and cut 24 triangles, shading from coral at outside to aqua at center point, and 24 shading from aqua at outside to coral at center point. (See Diagram 3 for triangle placement.)

5. Follow Diagram 4 to make 16 blocks. Follow Diagram 5 to make 48 blocks.

6. Join pieced blocks as shown in quilt diagram to make an 8-block-by-2-block vertical row. Repeat to make 3 more rows.

7. Cut 2 (2½" x 45") strips each on straight grain from lt. aqua, dk. aqua, lt. coral, med. coral, and dk. coral. Cut 4 (2½" x 45") strips from purple print. Join long edges of purple print, lt. aqua, dk. aqua, lt. coral, med. coral, dk. coral, and purple print strips to make 2 (7-color) bands. Cut across bands to make 24 (2½"-wide) multicolor strips. Join 8 strips to make 1 sashing strip. Repeat twice. Join rows with sashing strips.

8. Quilt as desired. Bind with paisley print fabric.

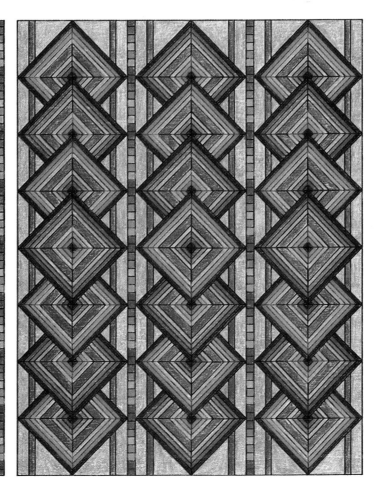

Woven Wonder

Here is another banded beauty, this one stitched by Judy Rankin. For an easy solution to piecing this awesome block, which I designed with inspiration from a graphic puzzle, follow the step-by-step diagrams. Six coordinated aqua fabrics weave in and out of mitered pastel frames.

Finished Size: 82" x 102"
Perimeter: 368"
Blocks: 10 (18" x 20") A blocks
10 (20" x 22") B blocks

Fabric Requirements:

Dk. rose print	1¾ yards
Rose print #1	2 yards
Rose print #2	1⅝ yards
Rose print #3	1⅝ yards
Rose print #4	1⅝ yards
Dk. aqua	⅞ yard
Lt. aqua	⅞ yard
Aqua print #1	⅞ yard
Aqua print #2	⅞ yard
Aqua print #3	⅞ yard
Aqua print #4	⅞ yard
Backing	6 yards
Aqua print for binding	⅞ yard

Pieces to Cut:

R7	98	dk. rose print
S3	80	dk. rose print
	30	rose print #1
Q35	80	pieced rose stripe*
Trapezoid	40	pieced rose stripe*
6½" x 10½" rectangle		
	20	pieced aqua stripe*
6½" x 8½" rectangle		
	30	pieced aqua stripe*
2½" x 6½" rectangle		
	19	pieced aqua stripe*
6½" square	8	pieced aqua stripe*

*See Steps 1–4. Reverse template for half the pieces.

Quilt Construction:

1. To make trapezoid template, extend template Q35 from corner dots 3" and place on fold (see template).
2. Cut all remaining print fabric into 1½"-wide strips crosswise.
3. Join 1½"-wide strips of rose prints #1–4 in order shown in photograph to make 4½"-wide bands. Cut Q35 and trapezoid pieces from these bands.
4. Join 1½"-wide strips of 6 aqua prints and solids in order shown in photograph to make 6½"-wide bands. Cut 6½" x 10½", 6½" x 8½", 2½" x 6½", and 6½"-square pieces from these bands.
5. Make 10 A blocks and 10 B blocks, following Diagrams 1 and 2. Make 5 strips from R7 and S3 pieces and 2½" x 6½" pieced strips, following Diagram 3 on page 76.
6. To make Row 1, join 2 A blocks, 2 B blocks, and 1 pieced strip as shown in Diagram 3. Repeat process to make Rows 3 and 5. To make bottom border, piece strip as shown and join to bottom of Row 5 (see Diagram 4 on page 76).
7. Join blocks and strips as shown in Diagram 3 to make Rows 2 and 4.
8. Lap-quilt rows as desired.
9. Follow Diagram 4 to join rows (see Block-to-Block Connections, page 121). Bind with aqua print.

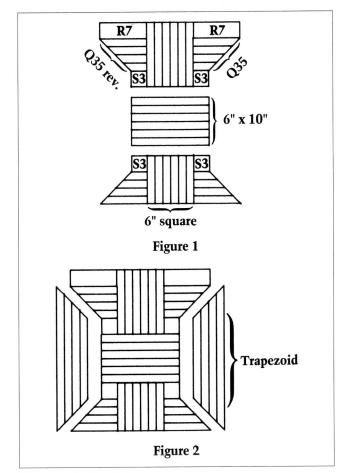

Diagram 1: Block A

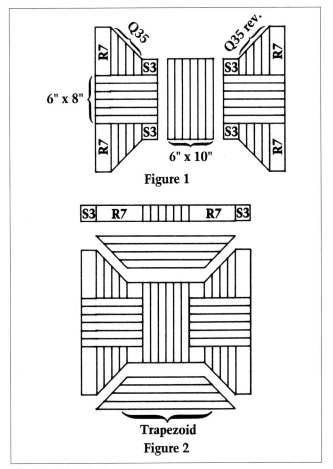

Diagram 2: Block B

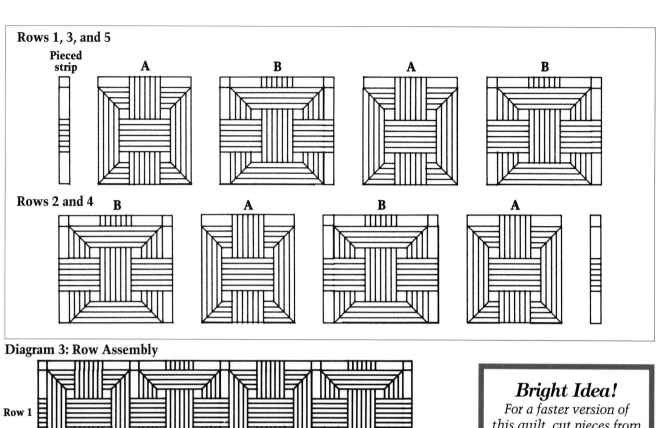

Rows 1, 3, and 5

Pieced strip

A   B   A   B

Rows 2 and 4

B   A   B   A

Diagram 3: Row Assembly

Row 1

Row 2

Row 3

Row 4

Row 5

Bottom border

Diagram 4: Quilt Assembly

Bright Idea!
For a faster version of this quilt, cut pieces from preprinted striped fabric instead of pieced bands.

Strawberries and Strings Vest

Using a variation of the *Woven Wonder* block, create a zippered vest. These instructions are for a medium size. Increase or decrease at the side edges of the block for larger or smaller sizes.

Material Requirements:

Dk. green print	¼ yard
Red print	¼ yard
Yellow print	¼ yard
White	¼ yard
Strawberry print	¼ yard
Black print	⅛ yard
Large gray print	⅛ yard
3 small gray prints	⅛ yard each
Lining	¾ yard
Strawberry print for binding	⅜ yard
1"-wide elastic	1 yard
⅛"-wide satin ribbon	12" red
	12" yellow
	12" green

20" separating zipper

Pieces to Cut:

Q35	8 pieced stripe
R7	16 strawberry print
S3	16 strawberry print
Trapezoid	4 pieced stripe
6½" x 10½" rectangle	2 black/gray stripe
6½" x 8½" rectangle	4 black/gray stripe
2½" x 6½" rectangle	4 black/gray stripe
2½" x 3" rectangle	2 strawberry print

Vest Construction:

1. Follow Steps 1–4 for *Woven Wonder* quilt, page 75, substituting fabrics in Material Requirements for rose and aqua fabrics.

2. Following diagram below, make 1 block (shaded area) for back and 2 half-blocks (unshaded areas) for front. (*Note:* Add ¼" seam allowance to half trapezoids when cutting.)

3. Join vest front and back sections at side seams (see diagram). Trim blocks to make neck edge and armholes as shown in diagram.

4. Separate zipper. With teeth pointing away from edge of vest, place bottom of zipper 2¼" from bottom of vest and stitch zipper to center front.

5. With right sides facing, lay vest on top of lining fabric, aligning front edges of vest with grain of lining fabric. Sew lining to vest along bottom and front, stopping 2" from bottom. Trim lining fabric even with vest. Turn and press. Topstitch across bottom of vest.

6. For button tab at waist, trim 1 end of each 2½" x 3" rectangle to a point. With right sides facing, sew tab along sides and point, leaving opening on straight end. Turn and press. Work buttonhole near pointed end (see photograph).

7. Make casing along bottom of vest by stitching in-the-ditch along first horizontal seam line in blocks at bottom of vest (see diagram).

8. Stitch raw edge of tab to 1 end of elastic. Attach safety pin to other end of elastic. Thread elastic through casing, safety pin first. Remove safety pin and stitch free end of elastic in place through seam allowances at front edge of vest. Stitch tab in place through seam allowances at opposite edge of vest. Sew button in place.

9. With right sides facing, join vest front to back at shoulder seams, leaving lining shoulder seams free. Turn under seam allowances on lining shoulder seams and slipstitch together. Bind neck edge and armholes with strawberry print fabric.

10. Using strawberry cutouts from print fabric, make 3 stuffed strawberries. Tie bow in 1 end of 1 length of ribbon. Tack bow to top of strawberry. Repeat with remaining ribbon for other 2 strawberries. Tie free ends of ribbons to zipper tab.

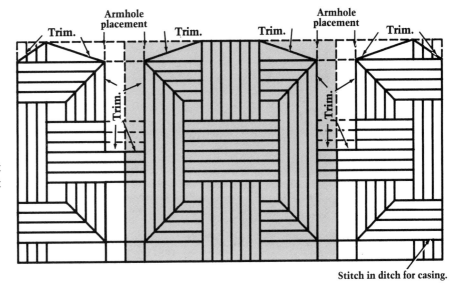

Vest Construction

Interlock

This intriguing design is a visual tongue twister. But its construction is simpler than it might seem. The entire quilt is made from just nine repetitions of one block. Add a series of two-inch borders for an intricate-looking puzzle that is sure to be a conversation starter.

Finished Size: 89½" x 97½"
Perimeter: 374"
Blocks: 9 (28½"-square) Interlock blocks

Fabric Requirements:

Print	6½ yards
White	6½ yards
Backing	8⅝ yards
Fabric for binding	1 yard

Pieces to Cut:

25" square	9 print
2½" x 31" strip	36 white
2½" x 26" strip	18 white
2½" x 36" strip	18 white
2½" x 6½" strip	4 white
2½" x 29" strip	18 white
	6 print

Quilt Construction:

1. Following Diagram 1, fold 1 (25") print square diagonally; press fold to crease. With square still folded, measure 2¾" from fold and mark. Measure 2½" from first marked line

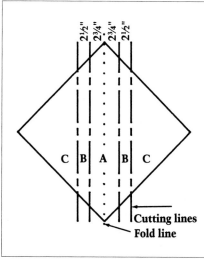

Diagram 1

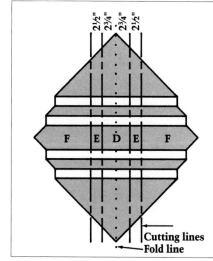

Diagram 3

and mark again. Cut along marked lines to make 5 sections as shown in Diagram 1.

2. With bias fabric against feed dogs, join a 2½" x 31" white strip to each side of section A (see Diagram 2, Figure 1).

3. Join a section B to each 2½" x 31" strip (see Diagram 2, Figure 2).

4. Join a 2½" x 26" white strip to each section B (see Diagram 2, Figure 3).

5. Join a triangle C to each 2½" x 26" strip (see Diagram 2, Figure 4). *

6. Following Diagram 3, refer to Step 1 above to cut pieced unit into 5 sections.

7. Join a 2½" x 36" white strip to each side of section D (see Diagram 4, Figure 1).

8. Join a section E to each 2½" x 36" strip (see Diagram 4, Figure 2).

9. Join a 2½" x 31" white strip to each section E (see Diagram 4, Figure 3).

10. Join a section F to each 2½" x 31" strip (see Diagram 4, Figure 4). * *

11. Trim pieced unit as shown in Diagram 4, Figure 4, to form a 29" square. (See Diagram 5 for finished block.)

12. Repeat Steps 1–11, to make 8 more blocks.

13. Following quilt diagram, join blocks. Join 2½" x 29" strips and 2½" x 6½" strips to make borders. Join borders to quilt top.

14. Quilt as desired. Bind.

  *Press seam allowances away from strips.
 * *Press seam allowances toward strips.

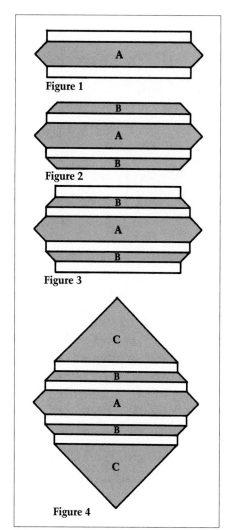

Figure 1

Figure 2

Figure 3

Figure 4

Diagram 2

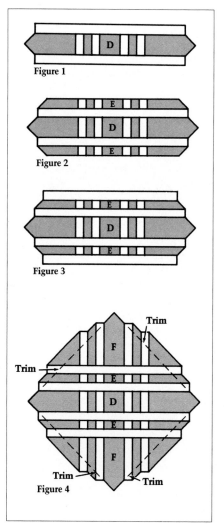

Figure 1

Figure 2

Figure 3

Figure 4

Diagram 4

Diagram 5

Manteca Ribbons

When the Manteca Quilters of Northern California asked me to design their raffle quilt, I went to work with enthusiasm. I used peach and navy fabrics to create striped bands that seem to overlap around the quilt's center square. Note how I used the reverse sides of the fabrics to provide subtle shading.

Finished Size: 108" x 108"
Perimeter: 432"

Fabric Requirements:

Navy	2½ yards
Navy print #1	1¾ yards
Navy print #2	1¾ yards
Navy print #3	1¾ yards
Navy print #4	2¾ yards
Peach	2 yards
Dk. peach print	2 yards
Lt. peach print	2 yards
Backing	9¼ yards
Navy for binding	1 yard

Pieces to Cut:

T37	36 striped band
	16 lt. peach print
	16 navy
	8 dk. peach print
	8 peach
	8 navy print #1
	8 navy print #2
T37A	8 navy
	4 lt. peach print
12½" square	4 lt. peach print
17½" square	1 navy
	4 navy print #4
2½" x 61" strip	4 navy print #1
(Group 1)	4 navy print #2
	4 navy print #3
	4 navy print #4
	4 dk. peach print
	4 peach
2½" x 25½" strip	12 navy print #1*
(Group 2)	12 navy print #2*
	12 navy print #3*
	12 navy print #4*
	12 dk. peach print*
	12 peach

2½" x 65" strip	8 navy print #1
(Group 3)	8 navy print #4
	8 dk. peach print
	8 peach

*Cut from reverse side of fabric.

Quilt Construction:

1. Following photograph for color placement, join Group 1 fabric strips to form 4 (6-stripe) bands. Join Group 2 fabric strips to form 12 (6-stripe) bands. Join Group 3 fabric strips to form 8 (4-stripe) bands. Following Diagram 1 for measurements, cut 4 pieces from Group 1 bands, adding ¼" seam allowance. Following Diagram 2 for measurements, cut 4 pieces from Group 1 bands and 8 pieces from Group 2 bands, adding ¼" seam allowance. (Reverse template for half of these.) From Group 3 bands, cut 36 T37 pieces for border.

2. Following quilt diagram and photograph for placement, join all pieces to make quilt top. Quilt as desired. Bind with navy fabric.

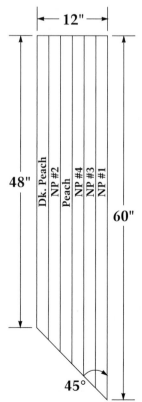

Diagram 1 (Make 4 from Group 1 fabrics.)

Piecing Suggestion: To complete piecing quilt top, join 1 rectangular unit to top of square, leaving final ¹/₂" of seam unstitched. Proceed counterclockwise to join remaining 3 rectangular units to center square. Join borders, mitering corners.

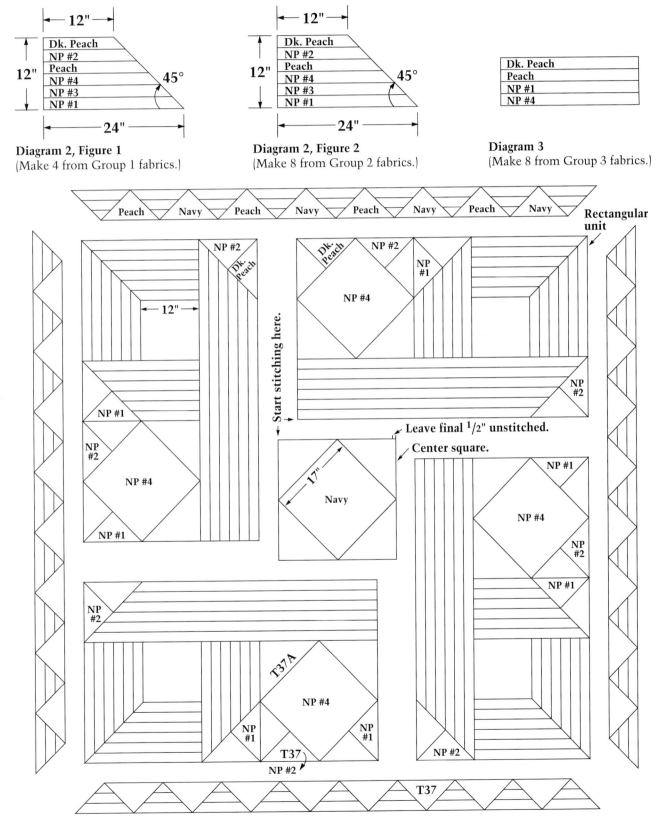

Diagram 2, Figure 1
(Make 4 from Group 1 fabrics.)

Diagram 2, Figure 2
(Make 8 from Group 2 fabrics.)

Diagram 3
(Make 8 from Group 3 fabrics.)

Baby Buggy Boomers

Many years ago, I received a small stack of string-pieced blocks, not enough to complete a quilt. They were from outdated fabrics, but I matched them with my current fabric supply to string-piece enough blocks, using pages from mail-order catalogs as foundations, for this baby quilt.

The buggy has a pocket for carrying an extra diaper, baby's favorite toy, or some other traveling necessity.

Finished Size: 68" x 74"
Perimeter: 284"
Blocks: 50 (7" x 10") string-pieced
  blocks
  3 (11"-square) string-pieced
    buggy blocks
  1 (11"-square) appliquéd
    buggy handle block
  2 (11½" x 13½") appliquéd
    wheel blocks

Fabric Requirements:

Scraps for strings	4½ yards total
Pink print	1⅛ yards
Pink stripe	2 yards
White rickrack	¾ yard
Narrow white piping	1½ yards
Black bias tape (½" wide)	
	5 yards
Backing	6¾ yards
Pink stripe for binding	
	¾ yard

Pieces to Cut:

11½" square		3 pink print
11½" x 13½" rectangle		
		2 pink print
1½" x 14½" strip		2 pink stripe
1½" x 21½" strip		2 pink stripe
1½" x 70½" strip		2 pink stripe
2½" x 23½" strip		4 pink stripe
2½" x 22½" strip		2 pink stripe
2½" x 70½" strip		2 pink stripe

Quilt Construction:

1. To make string-pieced blocks, you will need 53 sheets of paper for stabilizers. (Pages from old catalogs work well.)

2. String-piece 25 blocks diagonally across rectangle, with strips running from upper left corner to lower right corner. (See Sew and Flip Method, page 122.) String-piece 25 more blocks in same manner, with strips running from upper right corner to lower left corner. Trim blocks to 7½" x 10½". Remove paper foundations.

3. To make templates for piecing buggy sections, use a compass to draw a quarter-circle arc on an 11" square of paper. Cut the 2 sections apart. Trace sections 3 times, adding ¼" seam allowance. Cut out templates. String-piece scraps onto quarter-circle templates. Using remaining templates, cut 3 pieces from pink print. Join 1 quarter-circle to each pink print piece to form 3 blocks, sandwiching in rickrack on 1 block and piping on 2 blocks (see photograph). Remove paper foundations.

4. To make pocket, use 1 string-pieced quarter-circle block with piping trim. To face pocket, with right sides facing, pin 1 (11½") pink print square to a string-pieced quarter-circle block with piping. Sew across side of block that will border appliquéd buggy handle block above it (see diagram). Turn and press. With right side of another 11½" pink print square facing wrong side of faced block, baste the 3 squares together along the 3 raw edges.

5. Cut a 12" piece of black bias tape and appliqué to remaining 11½" pink print square to form handle (see diagram for placement).

6. Set the 4 buggy blocks together (see photograph and quilt diagram for placement). Two blocks with piping should be on bottom; handle block and block with rickrack should be on top.

7. To make buggy wheel blocks, use remaining black bias tape to appliqué free-form wheels to 11½" x 13½" rectangles (see photograph). Join buggy wheel blocks to bottom of buggy.

8. Join 4 string-pieced blocks, 2 across and 2 down, having all diagonals radiating from center of 4-block unit (see diagram). Join 1 (1½" x 14½") strip to each side of unit. Join 1 (2½" x 22½") strip to top of unit. Join this unit to top of baby buggy unit.

9. Join 6 string-pieced blocks, 2 across and 3 down. Join 1 (1½" x 21½") strip to each side of unit. Join 1 (2½" x 22½") strip to bottom of unit. Join unit to bottom of buggy unit as shown in diagram.

10. Refer to quilt diagram to make 2 panels of string-pieced blocks, 2 across and 10 down. Attach 1 (1½" x 70½") strip to inside of each unit. Attach 1 (2½" x 70½") strip to outside of each unit. Attach 1 (2½" x 23½") strip to top and bottom of each unit (see diagram).

11. Machine-quilt vertical panels with narrow zigzag stitching as desired. See Backing Accents, page 122, to join panels. Bind quilt with pink stripe fabric.

Log Lanterns

The Log Cabin quilt, an American favorite and a must for every quilt collection, is classic in style and often novel in color arrangement. The *Log Lanterns* quilt is made from two block designs. Blocks are set together with like colors adjoining to form "lanterns."

Karen Pervier is the proud maker of this quilt. Wendy Crigger did the quilting.

Block A   **Block B**

Fabric key
▨ Red
▧ Green
☐ White

Finished Size: 60" x 90"
Perimeter: 300"
Blocks: 20 (10"-square) A blocks
          20 (10"-square) B blocks

Fabric Requirements:

Red	2 yards
Green	2 yards
White	4 yards
Border print	2¾ yards
Backing	6 yards
Green for binding	⅞ yard

Pieces to Cut:

S3	40 green
5½" x 50½" border strip	2 border print
5½" x 90½" border strip	2 border print

Quilt Construction:

1. Cut each color in continuous 1½"-wide strips down length of fabric. Following quilt block diagrams, make 20 A blocks and 20 B blocks. As you join each color to center square (S3), trim strip to desired length, building around center square.
2. Following quilt diagram for color placement, set blocks together in 5 rows of 8 blocks each. Join rows.
3. Join 5½" x 50½" border strips to top and bottom of quilt. Join 5½" x 90½" border strips to sides of quilt.
4. Quilt as desired. Bind with green fabric.

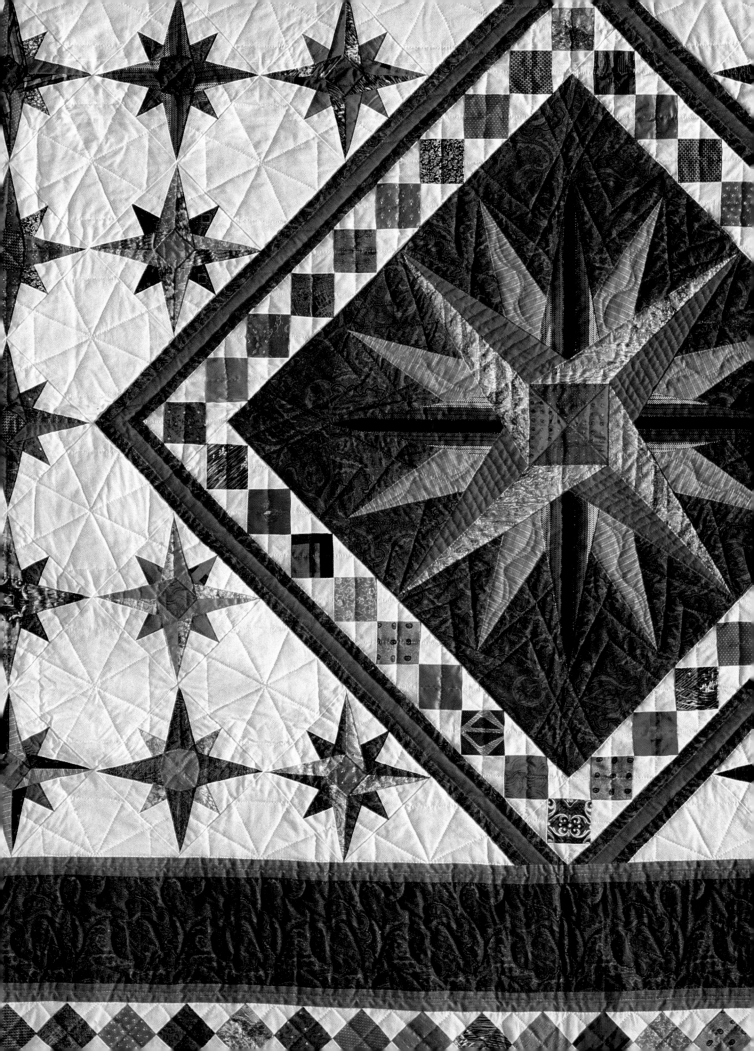

WARM THE WALLS

Quilts take on star status when they appear on the walls of banks, corporate offices, car dealerships, and even hospitals.

Golden Threads, Silver Needles II

Golden Threads, Silver Needles I

When the president of a bank in my hometown of Hendersonville, North Carolina, asked me to design a quilt to decorate the bank's new building, I was excited. By working closely with the architect and decorators, I was able to create a quilt that complemented the completed building's decor.

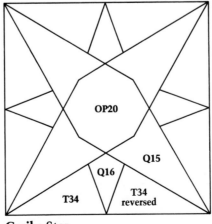

Caribe Star

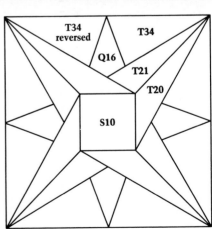

Split Star

Finished Size: 63" x 132"
Perimeter: 390"
Blocks: 28 (6"-square) Caribe Star blocks
24 (6"-square) Split Star blocks
1 (24"-square) Center Split Star block

Fabric Requirements:

White	3½ yards
Paisley	3¾ yards
Gold	⅜ yard
Rust	3⅝ yards
Assorted prints and solids	3⅝ yards total
Backing	8 yards
Paisley for binding	1 yard

Quilt Construction:

1. Follow block diagrams to make 1 Center Split Star block, 28 Caribe Star blocks, and 24 Split Star blocks. Make and join borders to Center Split Star block, as shown in quilt diagram.

2. Cut each 6⅞" square in half diagonally to make 32 side triangles. Cut 7¼" square into quarters diagonally to make corner triangles.

3. Follow quilt diagram to set center block, star blocks, and solid squares and triangles together.

4. Follow quilt diagram to add 3 inner borders by joining 1¼" strips and 6¼" strips to quilt, mitering corners.

5. Piece outer border and join to quilt.

6. Quilt as desired. Bind with paisley fabric.

Pieces to Cut:

OP20	28 assorted	T34	416 white*
OP32	4 paisley	T59/T60**	4 rust
OP33	16 paisley	6½" square	36 white***
Q15	112 assorted	6⅞" square	16 white***
Q16	208 assorted	7¼" square	1 white***
Q30	8 gold	⅞" x 32¼" strip	4 paisley
Q31	4 assorted	1¼" x 115½" strip	2 rust
S5	1 assorted	1¼" x 46½" strip	2 rust
S10	24 assorted	1¼" x 128½" strip	2 rust
S13	162 assorted	1¼" x 59½" strip	2 rust
T3	32 white	6¼" x 58" strip	2 paisley
T4	308 white	6¼" x 127" strip	2 paisley
T20	96 assorted		
T21	96 assorted		

*Reverse template for half the pieces.
**Join T59 and T60 to make 1 template.
***Cut edge of square on bias.

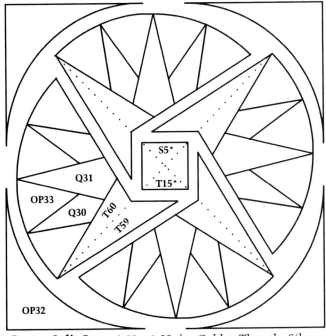

Center Split Star (*Use 1 S5 for *Golden Threads, Silver Needles I*; Use 4 T15 triangles for *Golden Threads, Silver Needles II*.)

Golden Threads, Silver Needles II

After I made *Golden Threads, Silver Needles I* for the bank in Hendersonville, I wanted a quilt like it for myself. So I made another one—but with a few changes.

Finished Size: 63" x 102"
Perimeter: 330"
Blocks: 14 (6") Caribe Star blocks
        18 (6") Split Star blocks
        1 (24") Center Split Star block

Fabric Requirements:

White	2⅞ yards
Paisley	3½ yards
Dk. red	1 yard
Red marbleized	⅜ yard
Lt. red	⅛ yard
Red/blue/black stripe	⅛ yard
Aqua	¼ yard
Assorted prints and solids	2 yards total
Red/blue stripe	2¾ yards
Backing	6 yards
Paisley for binding	⅞ yard

Pieces to Cut:

OP20	14 assorted
OP32	4 paisley
OP33	16 paisley
Q15	56 assorted
Q16	128 assorted
Q30	8 aqua
Q31	4 red/blue/black stripe
S10	18 assorted
S13	142 assorted
T3	32 white
T4	268 white
T15	2 dk. red
	2 lt. red
T20	72 assorted
T21	72 assorted
T34	256 white*
T59	4 dk. red
T60	4 red marbleized
6½" square	20 white**
6⅞" square	12 white**
7¼" square	1 white**
2¼" x 36½" strip	4 paisley/red pieced stripe
1¼" x 46½" strip	2 red/blue stripe
1¼" x 85½" strip	2 red/blue stripe
6¼" x 58½" strip	2 paisley
6¼" x 97" strip	2 paisley
1¼" x 59½" strip	2 red/blue stripe
1¼" x 98½" strip	2 red/blue stripe

  *Reverse template for half the pieces.
 **Cut edge of square on bias.

Quilt Construction:

1. Follow block diagrams on pages 90–91 to make 14 Caribe Star blocks, 18 Split Star blocks, and 1 Center Split Star block. Note that compass in Center Split Star block has been turned ⅛ of circle. Make and join pieced borders to Center Split Star.
2. Cut each of the 6⅞" squares in half diagonally to make 24 side triangles. Cut 7¼" square into quarters to make 4 corner triangles.
3. Follow quilt diagram to set center block, star blocks, and squares and triangles together.
4. Join inner borders to quilt in the order that they appear in quilt diagram and photograph, mitering corners.
5. Make outer pieced border. Join to quilt. Quilt. Bind with paisley fabric.

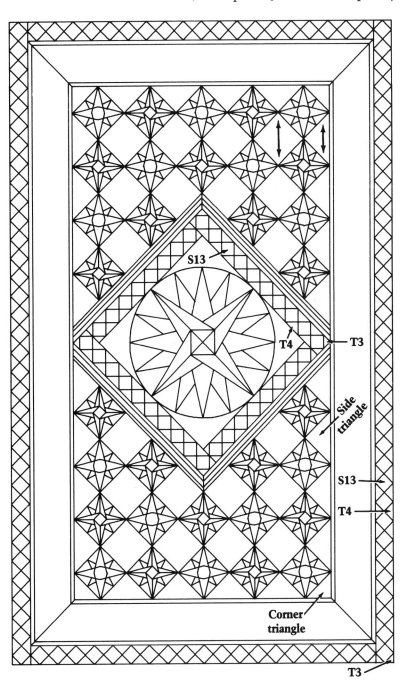

Car Star

A new car dealership nestled in the Blue Ridge Mountains is the setting for this quilted wall hanging. In this piece, the traditional Evening Star quilt block suggests a familiar industry logo. The sloping outlines of ancient mountains form the background. The old maxim—"A straight line is a line of duty; a curved line is one of beauty"—aptly describes this quilt.

Finished Size: 51⅜" x 54"
Perimeter: 210 ¾"
Blocks: 1 large star pentagon
        5 small star pentagons

Fabric Requirements:

Silver metallic	1 yard
Lavender	⅞ yard
Rose	½ yard
Assorted blues and greens	4 yards total
Backing	3⅜ yards
Blue for binding	¾ yard

Pieces to Cut*:

OP34	25 silver metallic
OP35	5 silver metallic
Q28	25 silver metallic
Q29	5 silver metallic
T7	25 lavender
T38	5 rose

* Refer to Steps 2–3 to cut remaining pieces.

Quilt Construction:

1. Follow quilt diagram to make 1 large star pentagon and 5 small star pentagons. Set aside.

2. To make full-size templates for flowing background, refer to Making Curved Templates, page 120. Draw a 51⅜" x 54" block on gridded freezer paper. (To make a sheet of paper large enough for pattern, overlap ends of paper and iron to make them adhere.) Referring to measurements on quilt diagram, draw large pentagon on block. Use flexible curve to draw curves as desired across entire block. Number templates in sequential order (the order in which you will join them). Indicate color and mark notches across curved seam lines. Cut out templates.

3. Iron numbered templates to wrong side of fabrics, referring to photograph for color placement or using colors of your choice. Cut out pieces, adding seam allowances. Extend notches and mark corners on seam allowances. Pin pieces together at corners and notches, remove freezer paper, and stitch.

4. Find midpoint of each 33⅜" side of pentagon and transfer 5 small pentagon measurements to these sides. Measure ¼" inside these and mark. Cut out pentagons on inside lines to form openings. Clip corners of openings. Set pentagons into opening.**

5. Use same method as in Step 4 to set large star pentagon in place.**

6. Layer backing, right side down; batting; and top, right side up. Quilt as shown in photograph or as desired. Bind quilt with blue fabric. Make and attach a casing to back of quilt for hanging.

**An alternate method for piecing this quilt is to leave flowing background intact and appliqué large and small pentagons in place. Then cut away background fabric from behind pentagons, leaving ¼" seam allowance.

Pastel Paisley Star

This and the remainder of the quilts in this chapter are part of more than 90 framed quilts that have come from all across the state of North Carolina to warm the walls of the obstetrics and gynecology unit of Duke University Hospital. It is an honor to be a part of this program to bring art into the hospital for the benefit of patients and their families, as well as the hospital workers.

Finished Size: 26" x 26"
Perimeter: 104"
Block: 1 (20"-square) Star block

Fabric Requirements:
Rose print	¼ yard
Paisley	¾ yard
Assorted pastel prints	1¼ yards
Backing	1 yard
Binding fabric (optional)	½ yard

Pieces to Cut:
C1	1 rose print
OP19	8 light print
Q36	8 paisley
S3	4 rose print
	44 assorted print
S10	8 rose print
	80 assorted print
T31	16 assorted print
1½" x 24½" border strip	
	4 paisley

Quilt Construction:

1. Referring to quilt diagram and photograph for color placement, arrange 16 assorted S10 squares into pieced block, placing rose square in 1 corner. Note how color arrangement forms stairstep pattern. Join squares. Repeat 3 times for 4 blocks.

2. Referring to quilt diagram and photograph for color placement, arrange 6 S10 squares and 4 T31 triangles into a pieced triangle. As in Step 1, note the stairstep pattern and place rose triangle at inside point of pieced triangle. Join pieces. Repeat 3 times for 4 pieced triangles.

3. Follow quilt diagram to piece center star, first joining OP19 pieces to Q36 pieces, stopping and backstitching at each corner dot. Then set in C1 circle.

4. Join stairstep triangles and then squares to pieced star.

5. Join paisley border strips to quilt, mitering corners.

6. Join assorted print and rose print S3 squares as shown in quilt diagram and photograph to make outer border. Join border to quilt.

7. Quilt as shown in photograph or as desired. Bind traditionally or see finishing tips on page 103.

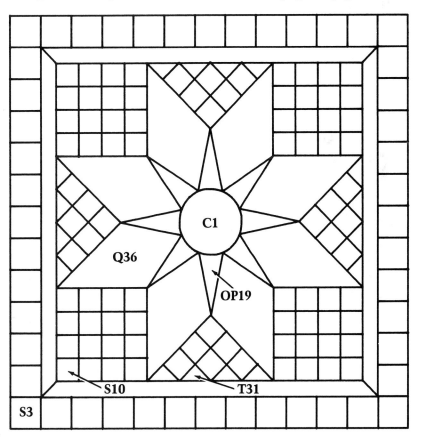

Split Star Variation

Splitting this simple star into dynamic shades of aqua creates movement—as if the star were turning silently within its black calico frame.

Finished Size: 28" x 28"
Perimeter: 112"
Block: 1 (12"-square) Split Star block

Fabric Requirements:

Dk. aqua print	⅜ yard
Lt. aqua print	⅜ yard
Peach print	½ yard
Black print	¼ yard
Lt. floral print	⅜ yard
Med. aqua print	¼ yard
Backing	1 yard
Binding fabric (optional)	½ yard

Pieces to Cut:

Q2	8 black print
S5	1 lt. floral print
T9	4 dk. aqua print
T15	4 lt. floral print
T53	16 peach print*
T57	8 lt. aqua print
T58	8 dk. aqua print
1½" x 22½" strip	4 black print
1" x 23½" strip	4 lt. aqua print
2½" x 27½" strip	4 lt. floral print
1" x 28½" strip	4 peach print
1½" x 30½" strip	4 med. aqua print
1¼" x 12½" strip	4 black print

*Reverse template for half the pieces.

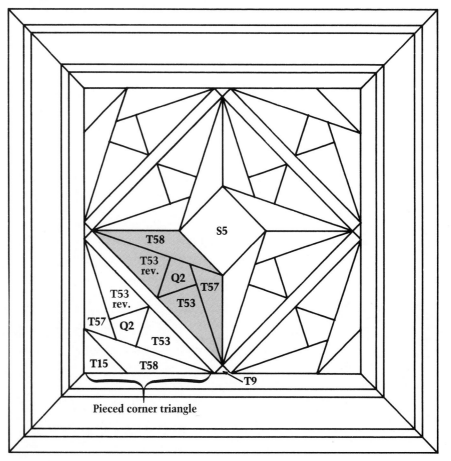

Pieced corner triangle

Quilt Construction:

1. Following shaded area of quilt diagram, join 1 Q2, 2 T53 triangles, 1 T57, and 1 T58. Repeat 3 times for 4 units. Join these units to S5 as shown in diagram, stopping at corner dots to allow for mitered angles, to complete Split Star block.

2. Join 2 (1¼" x 12½") black print strips to opposite sides of Split Star block. Join 1 dk. aqua print T9 triangle to each end of remaining 2 (1¼" x 12½") black print strips. Join strips to the remaining sides of Split Star block.

3. Following quilt diagram, make 4 pieced corner triangles. Join corner triangles to Split Star block.

4. Refer to quilt diagram and join borders, mitering all corners.

5. Quilt as shown in photograph or as desired. Bind quilt traditionally or see finishing tips on page 103.

Lavender Love

Repetition breeds content! Exotic though it appears, this overlapping star is easy to make using a repeating, pinwheel-type sequence. This miniature version of the *Manteca Ribbons* quilt takes advantage of pre-printed striped fabric for its points. The possibilities for varied fabric arrangements here are many!

Finished Size: 27" x 27"
Perimeter: 108"
Blocks: 1 (16"-square) Star block

Fabric Requirements:

Dk. lavender print	⅜ yard
Med. lavender print	⅛ yard
Lt. lavender print	⅛ yard
Med. green print	⅜ yard
Green stripe	½ yard
Lt. green print	¼ yard
Large floral print	¼ yard
Small black floral print	⅛ yard
Black print	¼ yard
Backing	1 yard
Binding fabric (optional)	½ yard

Pieces to Cut:

P6	8 lt. lavender print
P7	16 dk. lavender print
	8 lt. lavender print
	16 green stripe
	8 med. green print
	8 large floral print
Q23	4 green stripe
	8 med. green print*
Q25	4 green stripe
S3	4 med. lavender print
S11	8 lt. lavender print
	1 large floral print
T15	16 small black floral print
T64	12 dk. lavender print
2" x 22½" border strip	
	4 black print

*Reverse template for half the pieces.

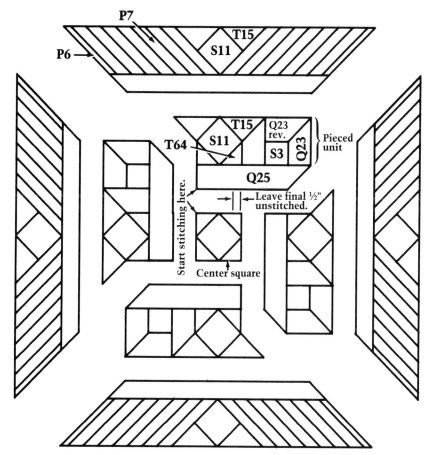

Quilt Construction:

1. Following quilt diagram and photograph, make center star block.

2. Join remaining S11 and T15 pieces to make 4 triangles for outer border as shown in quilt diagram. Follow quilt diagram to join P6 and P7 pieces for outer border. Join pieced border units to triangles. Join inner border strips to pieced border units. Attach borders to quilt.

3. Quilt as shown in photograph.

4. Bind traditionally or see finishing tips on page 103.

Piecing Suggestion

To complete piecing quilt top, join 1 pieced unit to top of square, leaving final ½" of seam unstitched. Proceed counterclockwise to join remaining 3 pieced units to center square. Join borders, mitering corners.

Car Star Variation

No two blocks alike, this quilt is a simple but happy version of the more advanced Car Star design. This one requires only a little concentration for a perfect block layout.

Finished Size: 28¼" x 29½"
Perimeter: 115½"
Blocks: 4 Star Pentagon blocks

Fabric Requirements:

Lt. floral print	1¼ yards
Black print	¼ yard
Yellow print	¼ yard
Rose print	¼ yard
Blue print	¼ yard
Purple print	¼ yard
Backing	1 yard

Pieces to Cut:

OP34	4 black print
	4 purple print
	4 yellow print
	4 blue print
	4 rose print
Q28	8 black print
	3 purple print
	3 yellow print
	3 blue print
	3 rose print
S3	1 purple print
	1 yellow print
	1 blue print
	1 rose print
T7	20 lt. floral print
T30	8 lt. floral print*
T68	4 lt. floral print*
	1 purple print**
	1 yellow print
	1 blue print**
	1 rose print
2½" x 26" strip	2 lt. floral print
2½" x 24¾" strip	2 lt. floral print

*Reverse template for half the pieces.
**Reverse template.

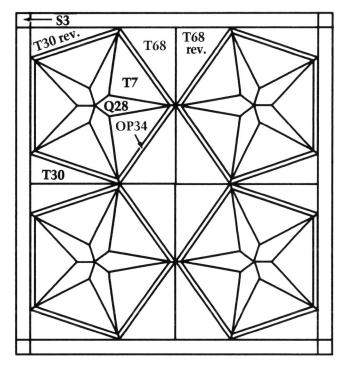

Quilt Construction:

1. Referring to quilt diagram and photograph for color placement, make 4 star pentagon blocks.

2. Continuing to refer to photograph for color placement, join blocks, 2 across and 2 down.

3. Join 1 (2½" x 26") strip to top and 1 to bottom of quilt.

4. Join 1 S3 square to each end of each 2½" x 24¾" strip. Join pieced strips to sides of quilt top.

5. Quilt as shown in photograph or as desired.

6. Trim batting and backing even with quilt top. With right sides together, sew a narrow (½") fabric strip to each side of wall hanging, sewing through all layers. Lay wall hanging on foam-core board (cut to same size as wall hanging). Fold raw edge of fabric extension in, then wrap extension over edge of foam-core. Secure fabric with sequin pins.

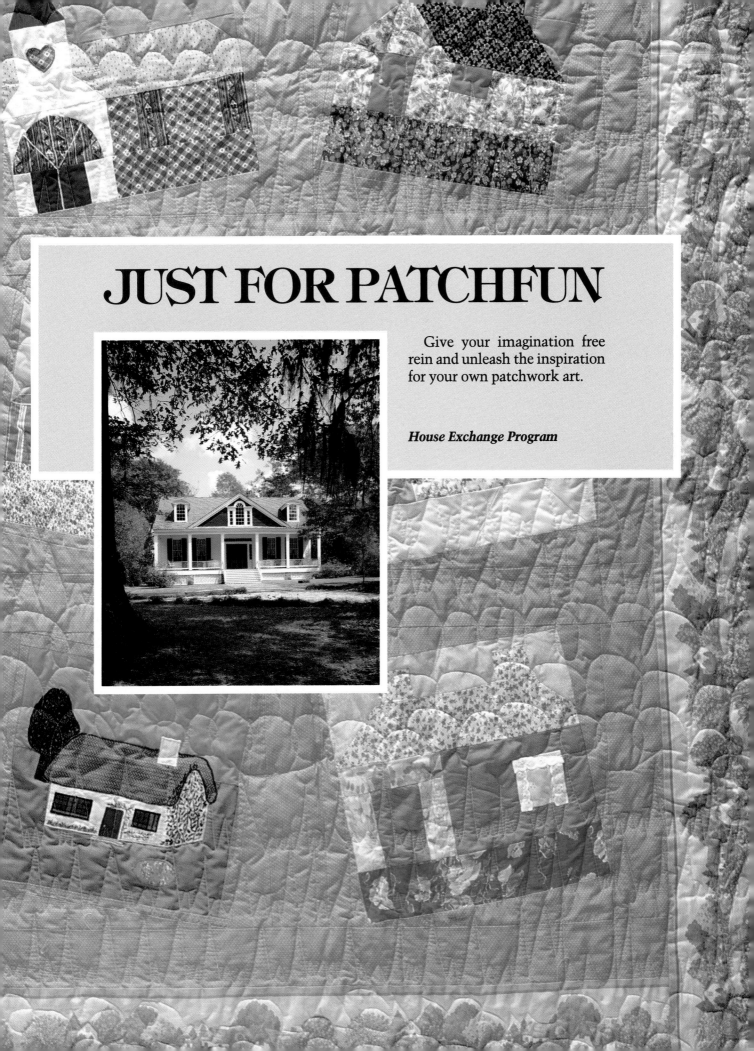

JUST FOR PATCHFUN

Give your imagination free rein and unleash the inspiration for your own patchwork art.

House Exchange Program

House Exchange Program

Sheila Scawen and several of her quilting friends in England joined my Freedom Escape quilt class in a block exchange to create this whimsical quilt.

Finished Size: 83" x 101"
Perimeter: 368"
Blocks: 20 (15"-square) House blocks

Fabric Requirements:

Assorted prints and solids	2¾ yards total
Blue pindot	2¼ yards
Border print	3 yards
Backing	6½ yards
Fabric for binding	⅞ yard

Pieces to Cut:
House block triangle*

	80 blue pindot
3½" x 15½" strip	25 blue pindot
3½" x 75½" strip	6 blue pindot
4½" x 79½" strip	2 border print
4½" x 97½" strip	2 border print

*See Step 1.

Quilt Construction:
1. To make house block triangle template, draw a 2³⁄₁₆" x 12¹³⁄₁₆" x 13" right triangle. Add ¼" seam allowances.

2. Design 20 (13½") house block center squares from drawings, photographs, or from your imagination. Use freezer paper (see Gridded Freezer Paper as a Creative Tool, page 120) to make templates for house blocks. Cut out pieces and make 13½" squares. Join 13½" edges of blue pindot triangles to edges of house blocks to tilt houses and to increase block size to 15½" (see quilt diagram for triangle placement).

3. Follow quilt diagram to join 3½" x 15½" sashing strips to opposite sides of blocks, creating 5 rows of 4 blocks each. Join rows with 3½" x 75½" sashing strips. Join remaining 3½" x 75½" strips to top and bottom of quilt (see quilt diagram).

4. Join border-print strips to edges of quilt as shown in quilt diagram.

5. Quilt as desired. Bind.

House block

House block triangles

Bright Idea!
Do you have an accumulation of odd-sized blocks looking for a special setting? Add borders to enlarge them to a uniform size. Then tilt them by adding triangles as shown in House Exchange Program.

Tea for Two Cozy

This tea cozy is large enough to cover not just the pot, but the entire tea service. The lining is made from silver cloth, a material that keeps silver from tarnishing.

To personalize this tea cozy for a wedding present, create a pieced block of the couple's first home on one side and appliqué a teapot in the bride's china pattern on the reverse side.

Finished Size: 16" x 19"
(excluding ruffle)
Blocks: 1 (16" x 19") House block
1 (16" x 19") Tea Set block

Fabric Requirements:

Navy print	1¾ yards
White	½ yard
Assorted prints and solids	⅜ yard total
Silver cloth	½ yard
Ruffled eyelet (1½"-wide)	1½ yards
Cotton batting	

Cozy Construction:

1. Copy a 16" x 19" house block from a photograph or draw your own design. Use freezer paper to make templates for house block (see Gridded Freezer Paper as a Creative Tool, page 120). Cut pieces from assorted prints and solids, adding ¼" seam allowance, and make block.

2. Cut silver cloth and 2 pieces of batting to match house block. Layer silver cloth, right side down; batting; and house block, right side up. Baste raw edges to secure all layers.

3. Hand-quilt house block as desired.

4. Enlarge Tea Set pattern on page 128 onto gridded freezer paper or draw your own design. Cut out templates.

Iron shiny side of templates to right side of white fabric. Cut out pieces, adding ¼" seam allowance. (For hand appliqué, turn under seam allowance and press.) Remove freezer paper. Cut a 16½" x 19½" rectangle from navy print. Appliqué tea set to rectangle. (See Appliqué Accents, page 121, for further instructions on machine appliqué.)

5. Cut silver cloth and 2 pieces of batting to match tea set block.

Layer silver cloth, right side down; batting; and tea set block, right side up. Baste the raw edges by hand to secure all layers. Machine-tack block at 1½" intervals.

6. Make a 6" x 102" ruffle strip from

navy print. Fold strip in half lengthwise with wrong sides facing and raw edges aligned. Gather to fit top and sides of cozy. Baste eyelet trim to raw edge of ruffle. With eyelet trim and ruffle facing right side of block and raw edges aligned, baste ruffle to tea set block.

7. With right sides facing and ruffle to the inside, stitch blocks together along top and side edges, leaving bottom edge open. Handstitch a 2"-wide bias strip of navy print over raw edges to bind top and side seams. Turn cozy right side out.

8. Cut a 3½" x 40" bias strip from navy print (piece if necessary) and bind bottom of cozy.

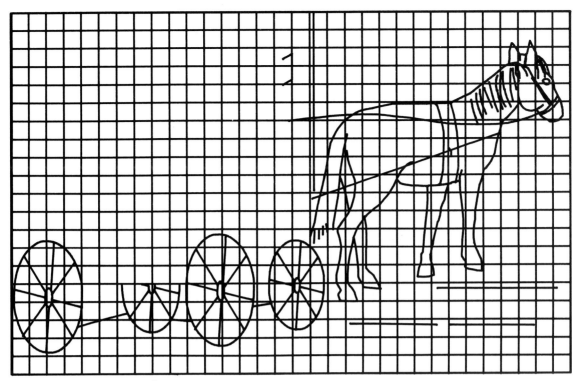

Horse and Buggy Quilting Pattern:
1 square = 1".

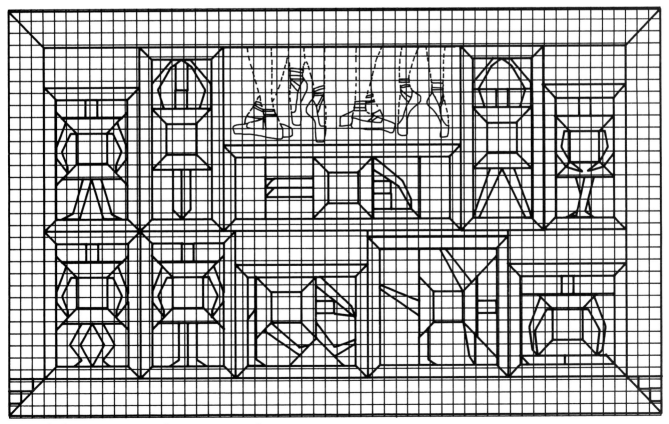

Spotlight Dancing Spools: 1 square = 1".

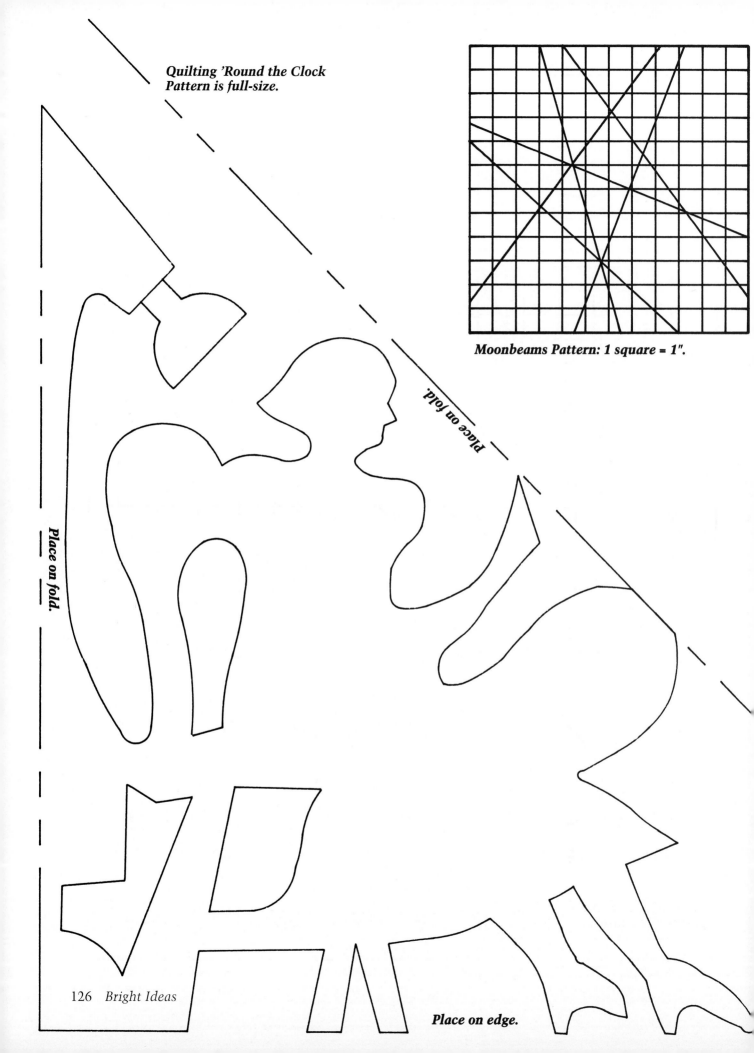

Quilting 'Round the Clock Pattern is full-size.

Moonbeams Pattern: 1 square = 1".

Place on fold.

Place on fold.

Place on fold.

Place on edge.

| 1¾" | 1¼" | ¾" | 1½" | | 1½" | | 1½" | ¾" | 1¼" | 1¼" | 1¼" | 1¼" | 1¼" | 1¼" | 1¼" | 9¼" |

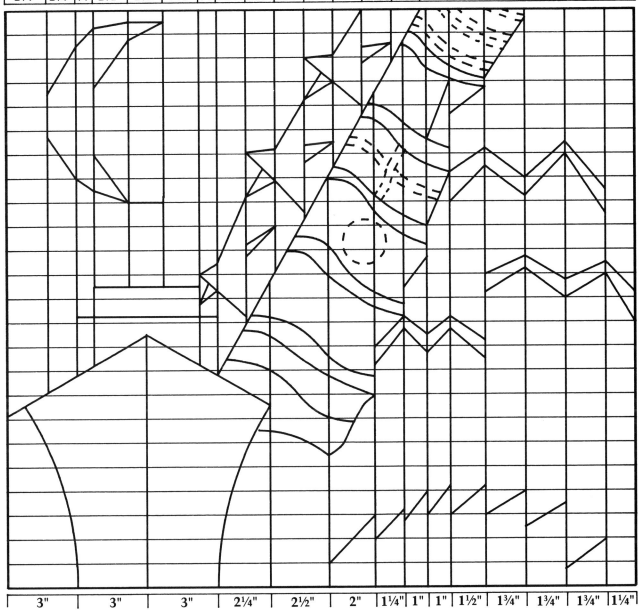

| 3" | 3" | 3" | 2¼" | 2½" | 2" | 1¼" | 1" | 1" | 1½" | 1¾" | 1¾" | 1¾" | 1¼" |

Cruise and Quilt Banner

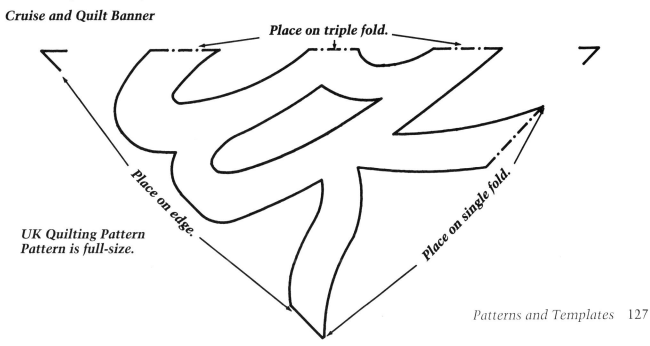

Place on triple fold.

Place on edge.

Place on single fold.

UK Quilting Pattern
Pattern is full-size.

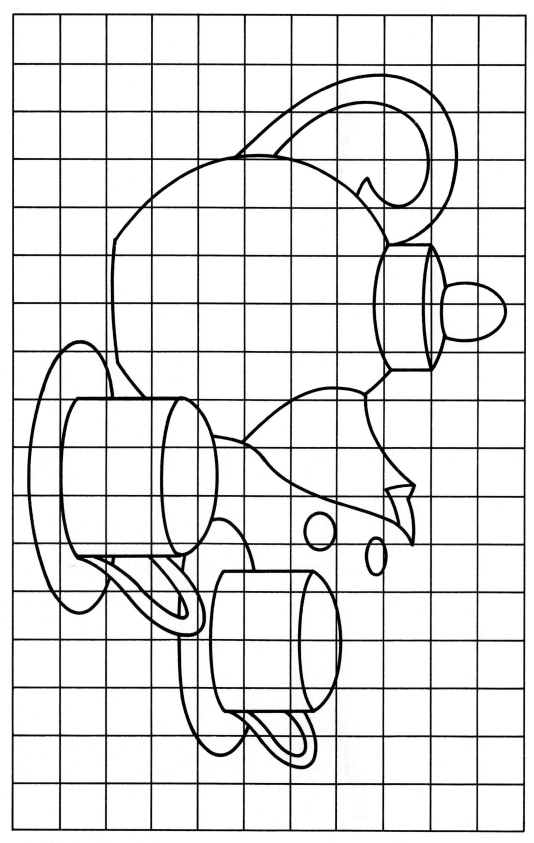

Tea for Two Cozy: 1 square = 1".

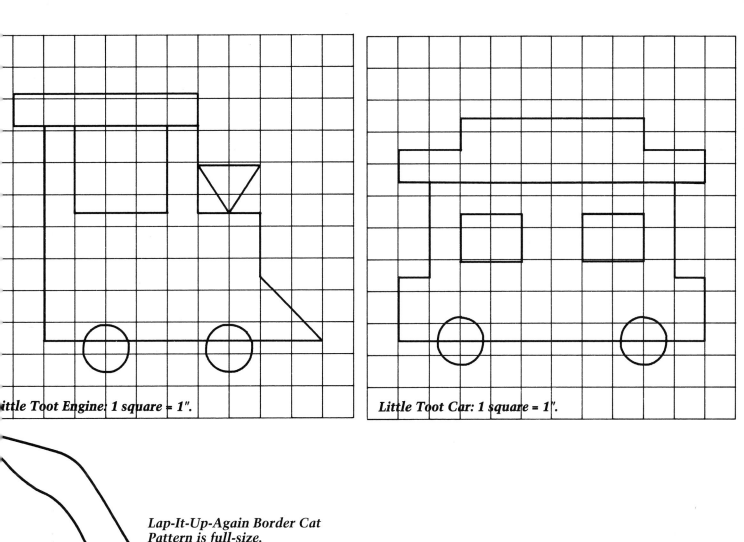

Little Toot Engine: 1 square = 1".

Little Toot Car: 1 square = 1".

Lap-It-Up-Again Border Cat
Pattern is full-size.

Moose Appliqué
Pattern is full-size.

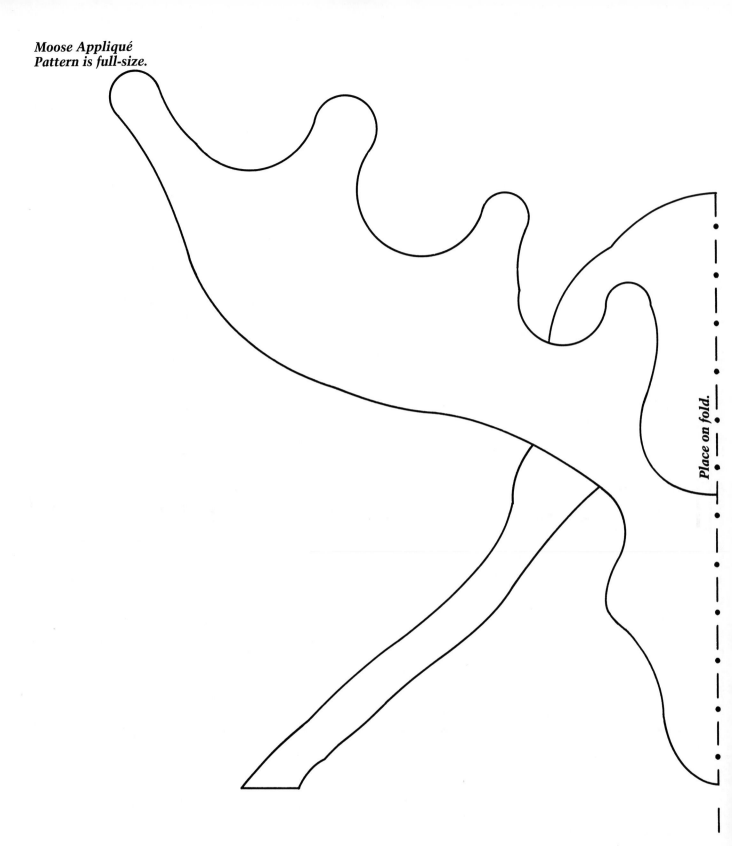

Place on fold.

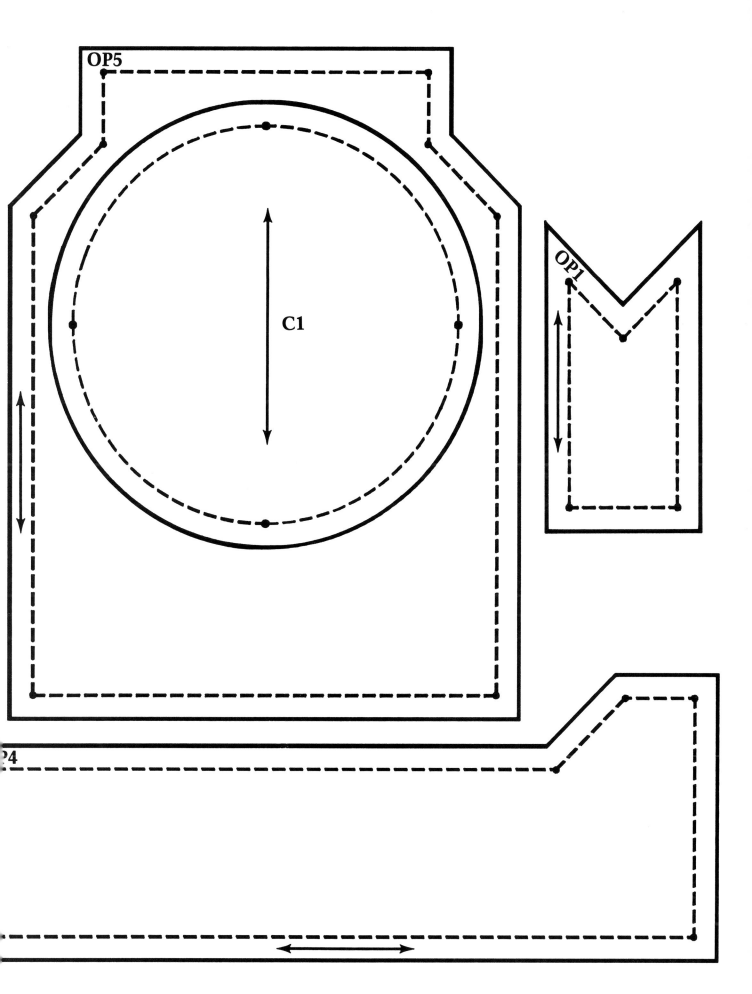

OP5

C1

OP1

P4

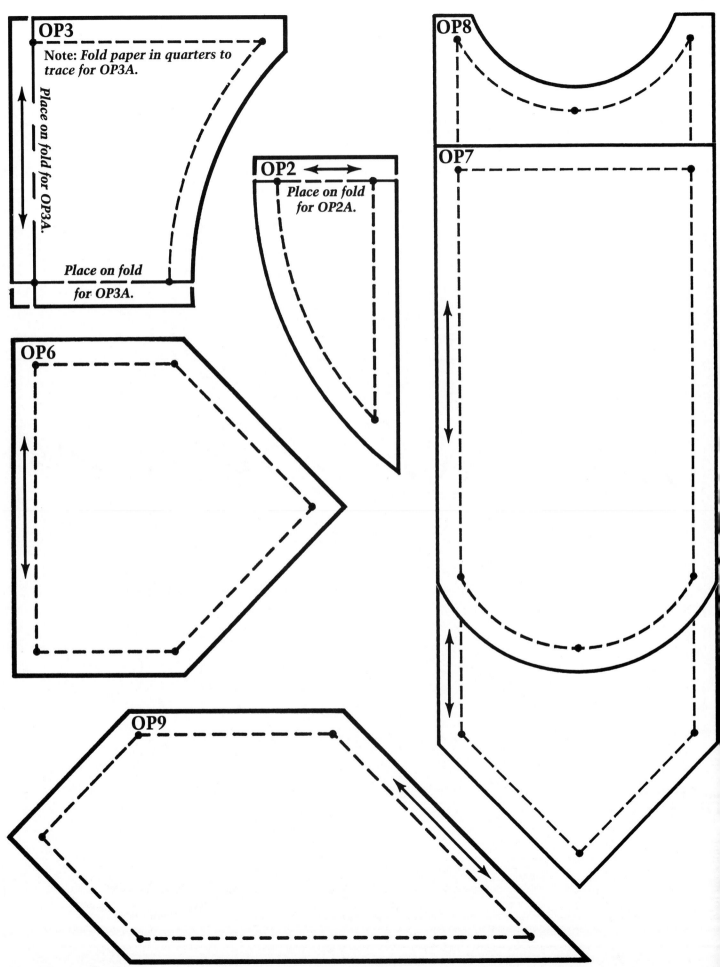

OP3

Note: *Fold paper in quarters to trace for OP3A.*

Place on fold for OP3A.

Place on fold for OP3A.

OP2

Place on fold for OP2A.

OP8

OP7

OP6

OP9

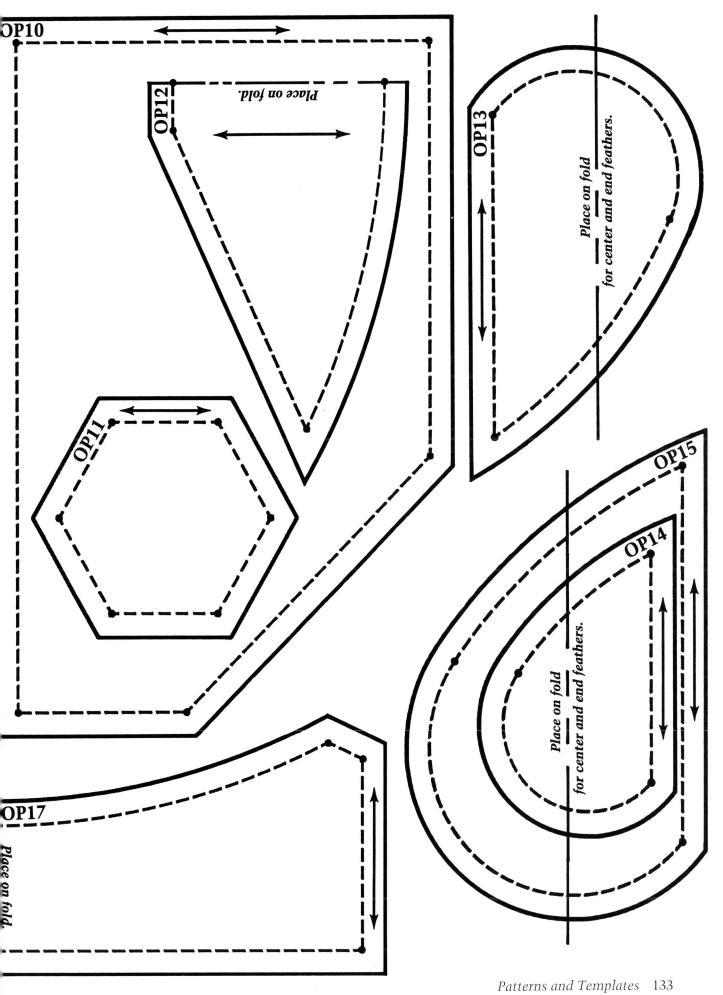

OP10

OP12

Place on fold.

OP11

OP13

*Place on fold
for center and end feathers.*

OP15

OP14

*Place on fold
for center and end feathers.*

OP17

Place on fold.

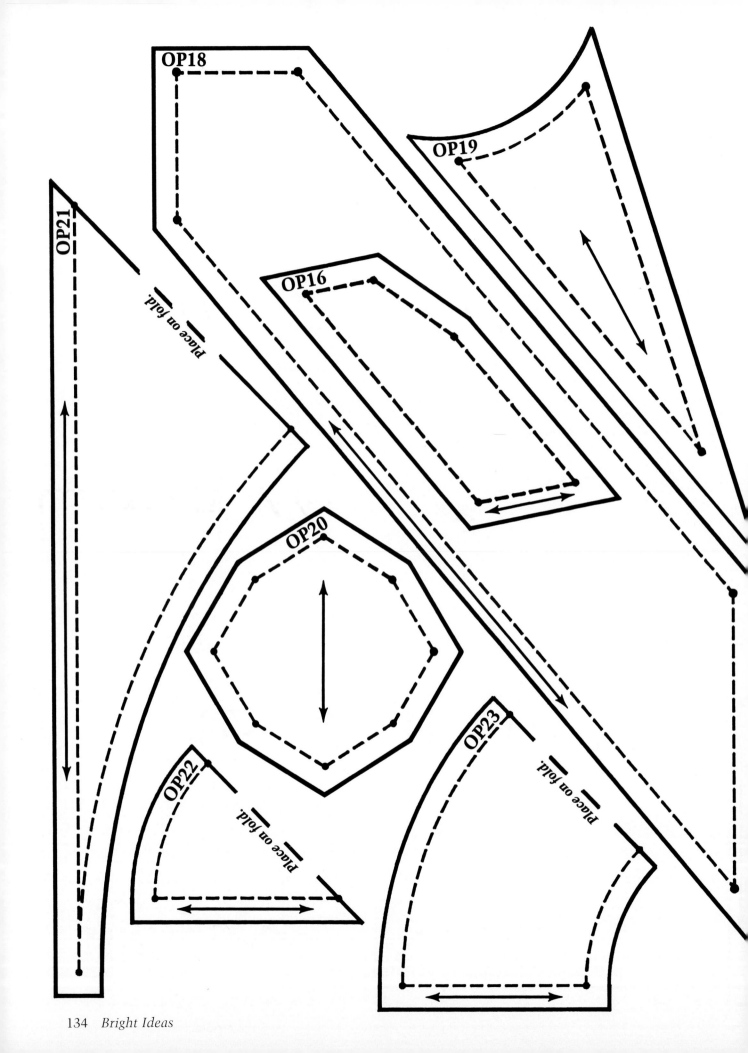

OP18

OP19

OP21

OP16

Place on fold.

OP20

OP22

Place on fold.

OP23

place on fold.

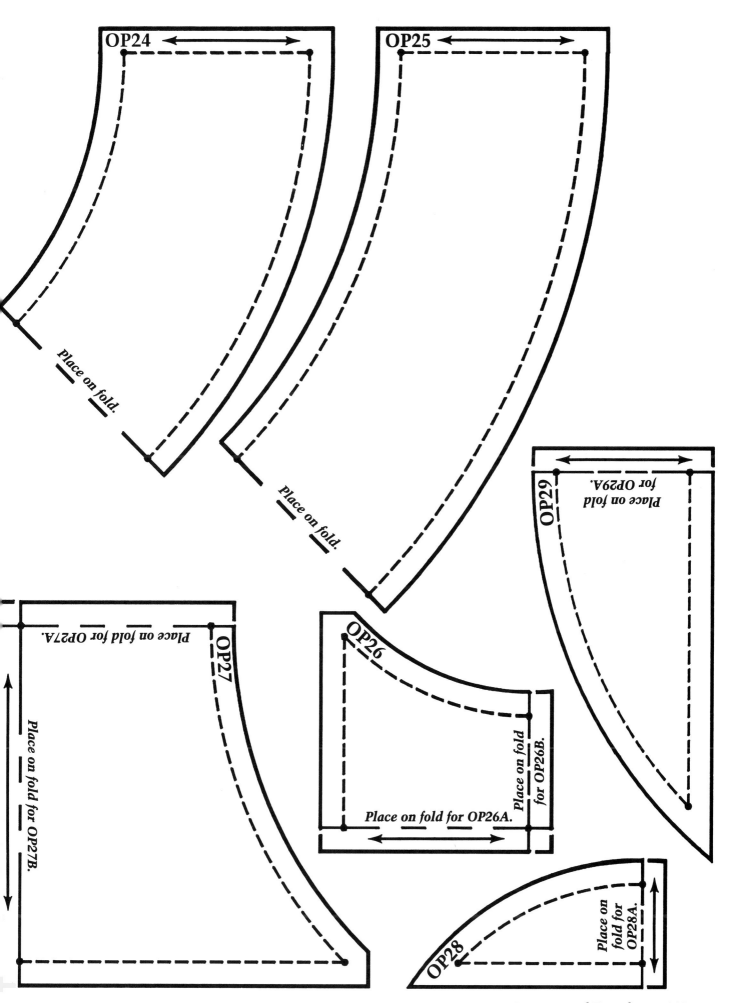

OP24

Place on fold.

OP25

Place on fold.

OP29

Place on fold for OP29A.

OP27

Place on fold for OP27A.

Place on fold for OP27B.

OP26

Place on fold for OP26B.

Place on fold for OP26A.

OP28

Place on fold for OP28A.

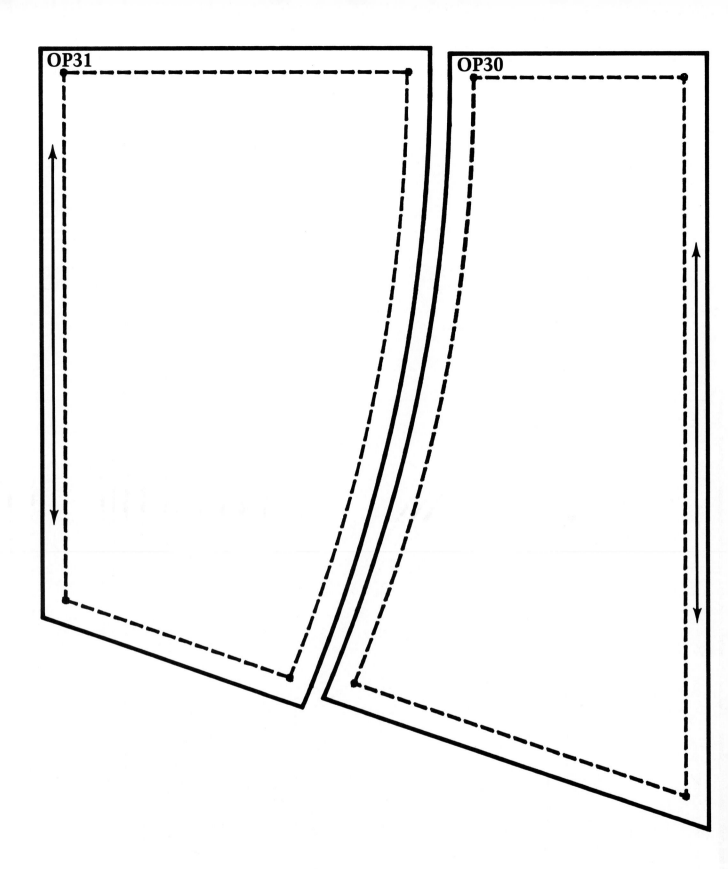

OP31

OP30

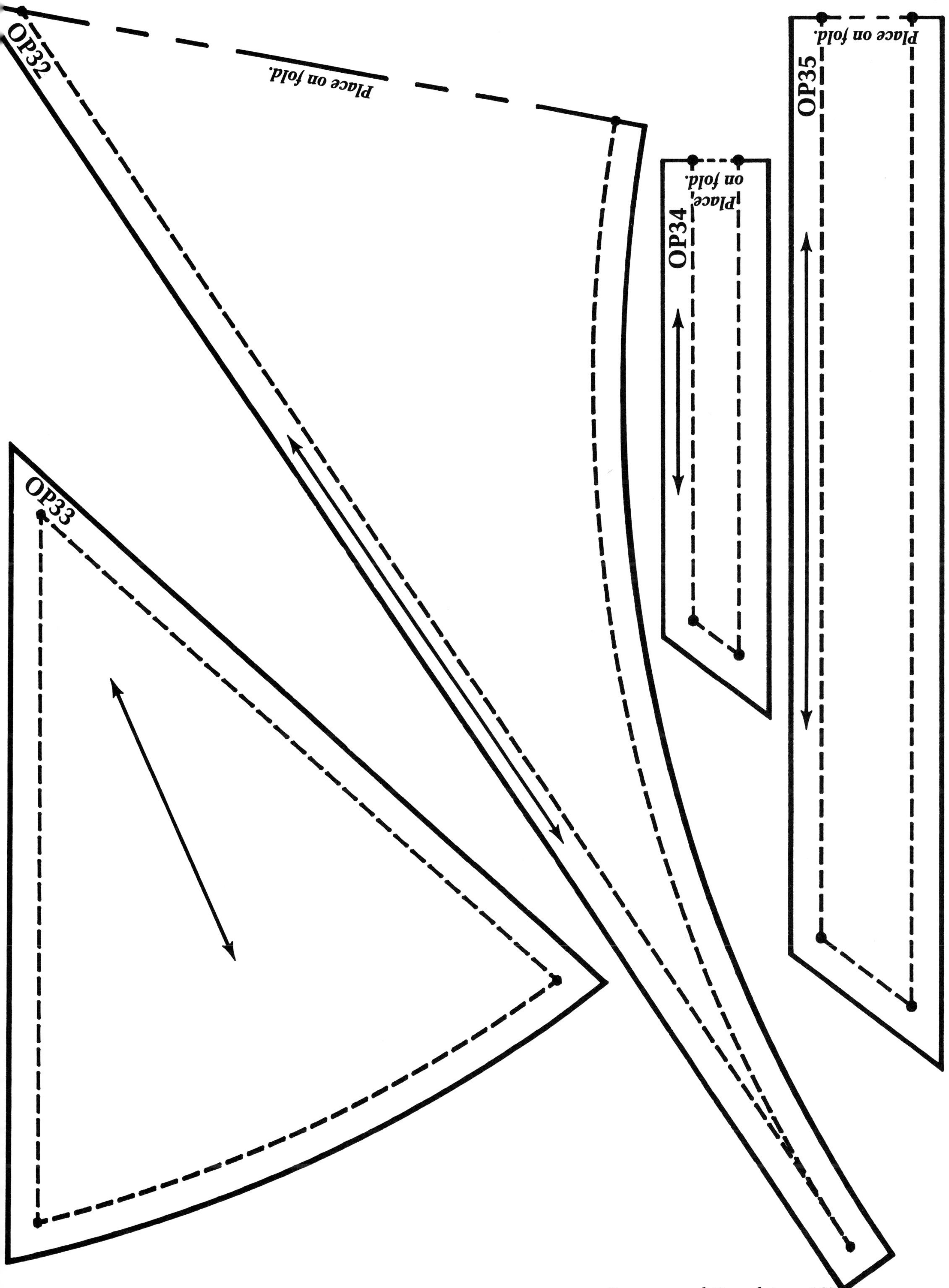

OP32

Place on fold.

OP33

OP34

Place on fold.

OP35

Place on fold.

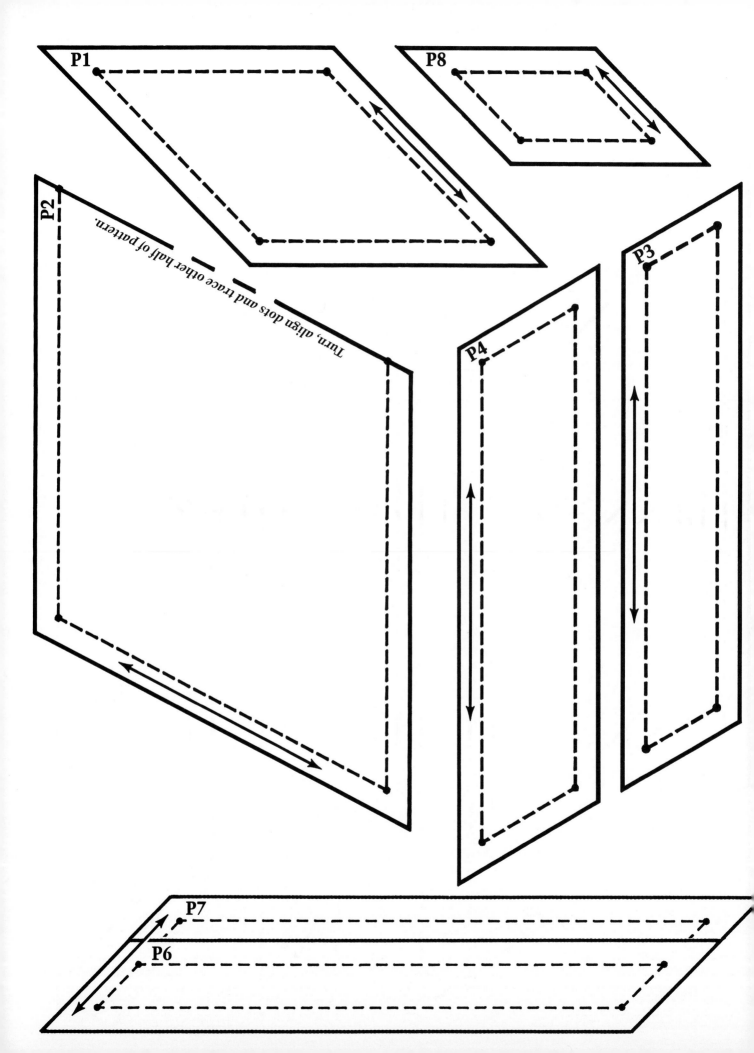

P1

P8

P2

Turn, align dots and trace other half of pattern.

P4

P3

P7

P6

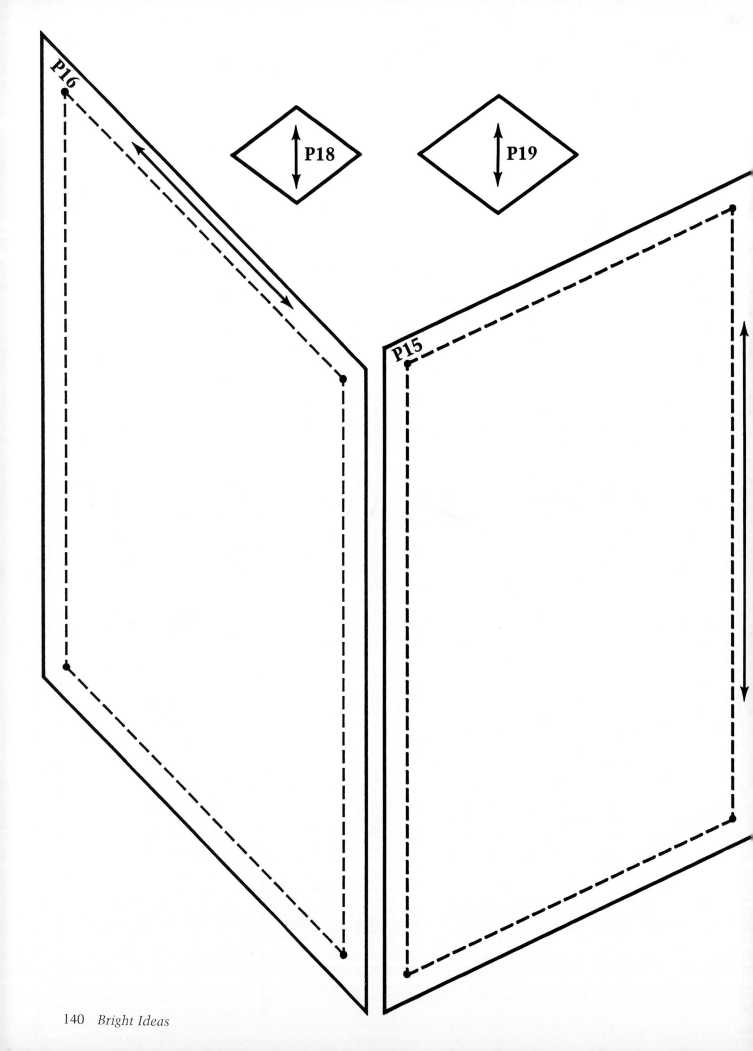

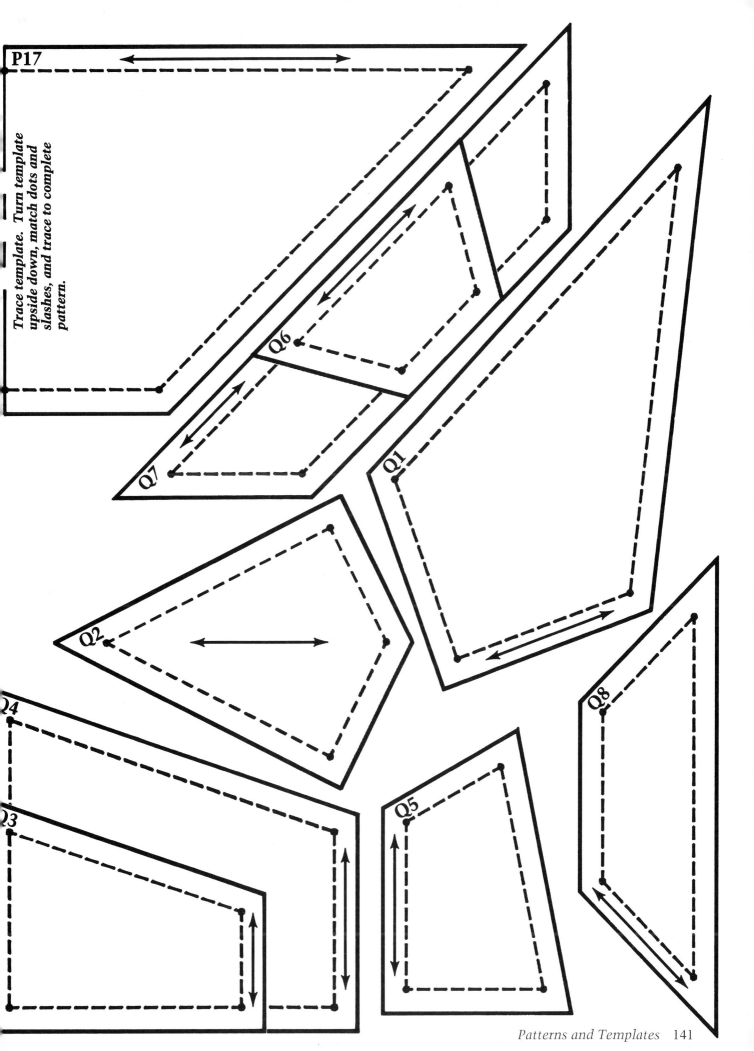

P17

Trace template. Turn template upside down, match dots and slashes, and trace to complete pattern.

Q6

Q7

Q1

Q2

Q4

Q3

Q8

Q5

Q9

Place on fold.

Q15

Q16

Q11

Place on fold.

Q13

Q14

Q12

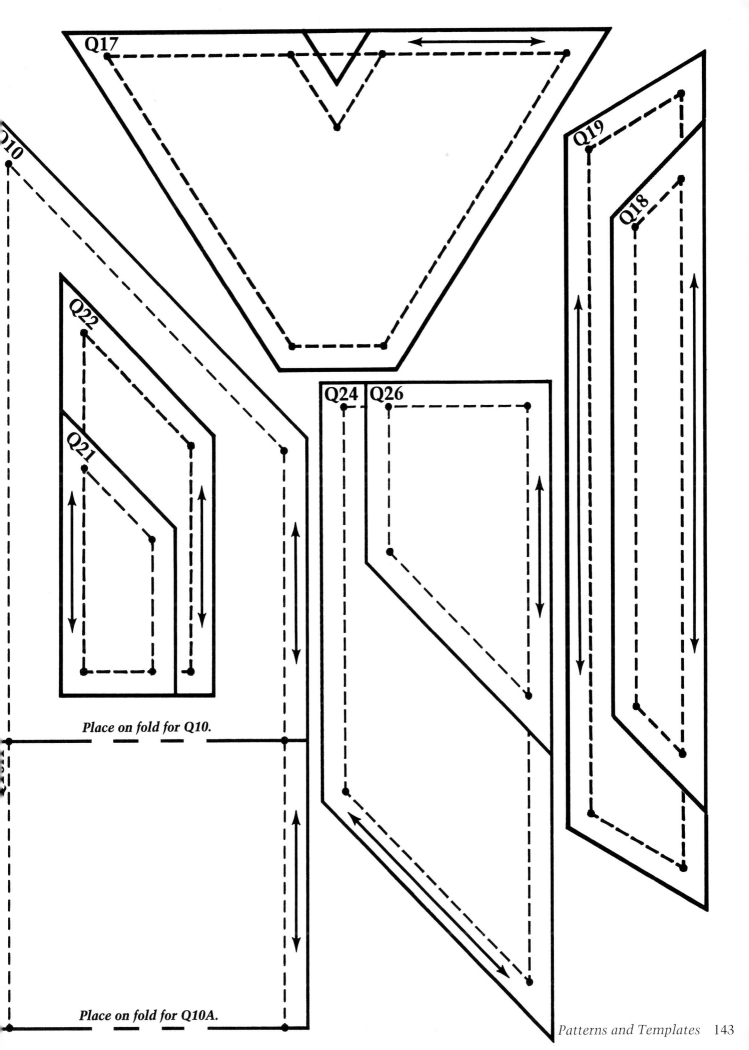

Q17

Q10

Q19

Q18

Q22

Q21

Q24 **Q26**

Place on fold for Q10.

Place on fold for Q10A.

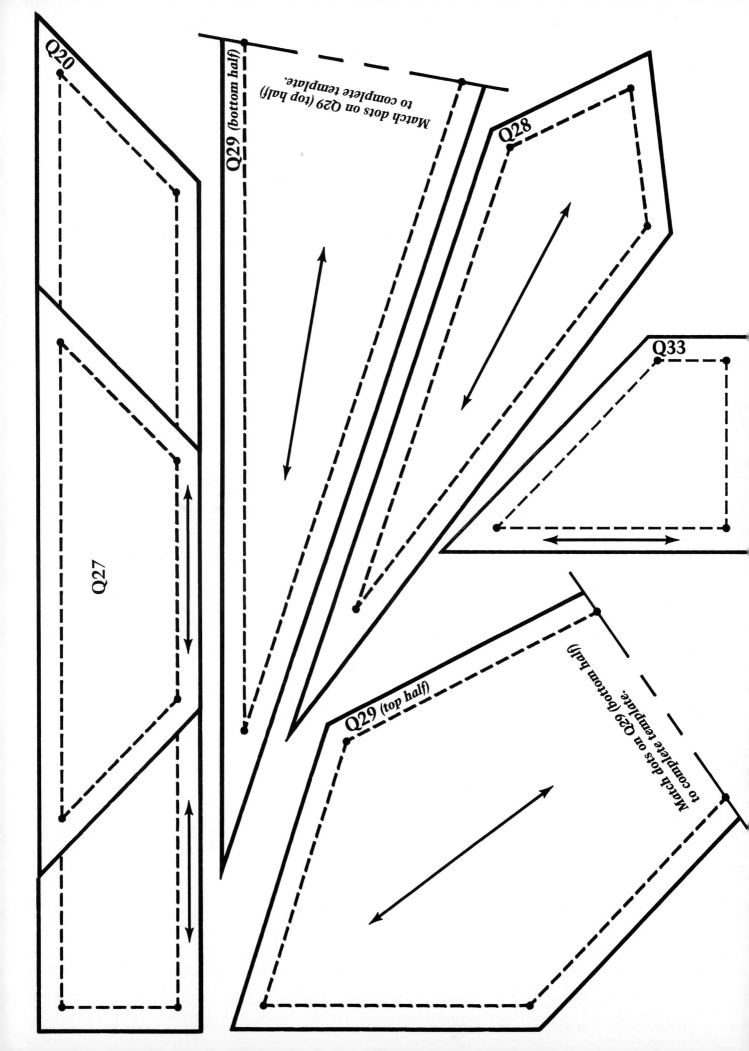

Q20

Q29 (bottom half)

Match dots on Q29 (top half)
to complete template.

Q28

Q33

Q27

Q29 (top half)

Match dots on Q29 (bottom half)
to complete template.

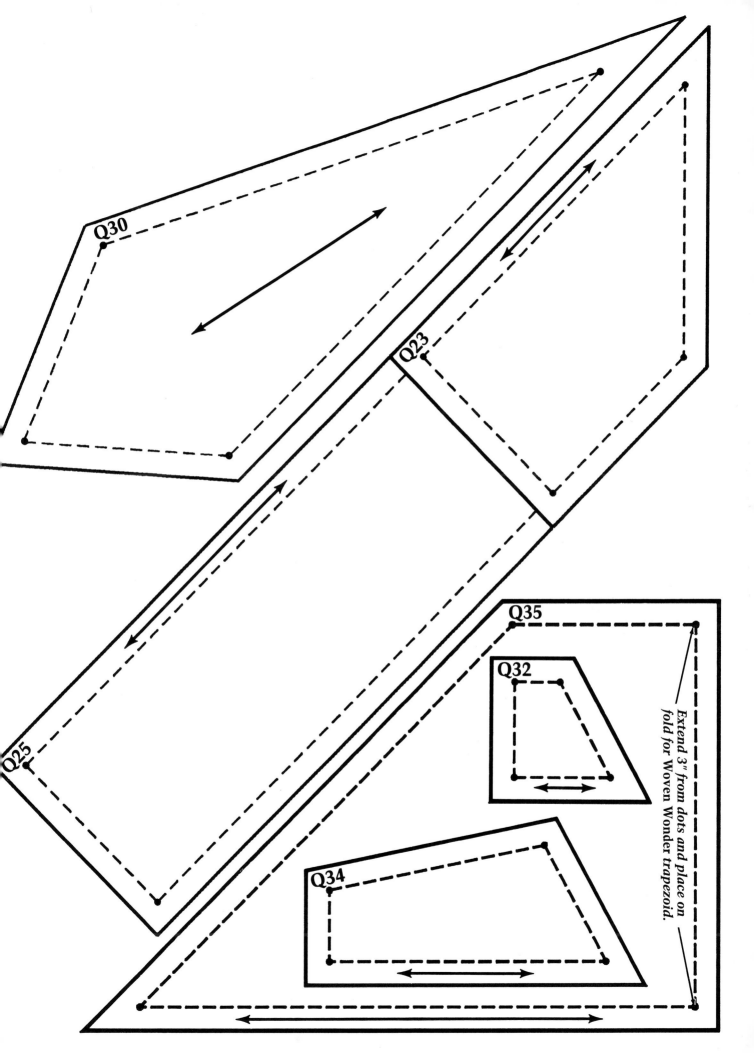

Q30

Q23

Q35

Q32

Q34

Q25

Extend 3" from dots and place on
fold for Woven Wonder trapezoid.

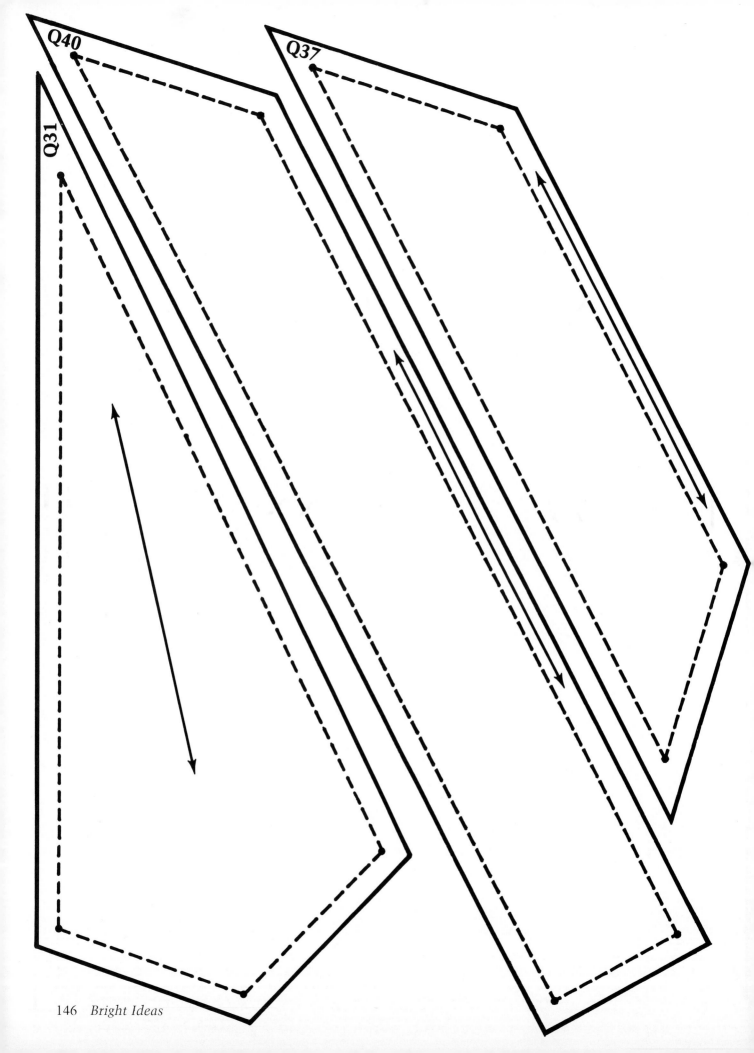

Q40

Q37

Q31

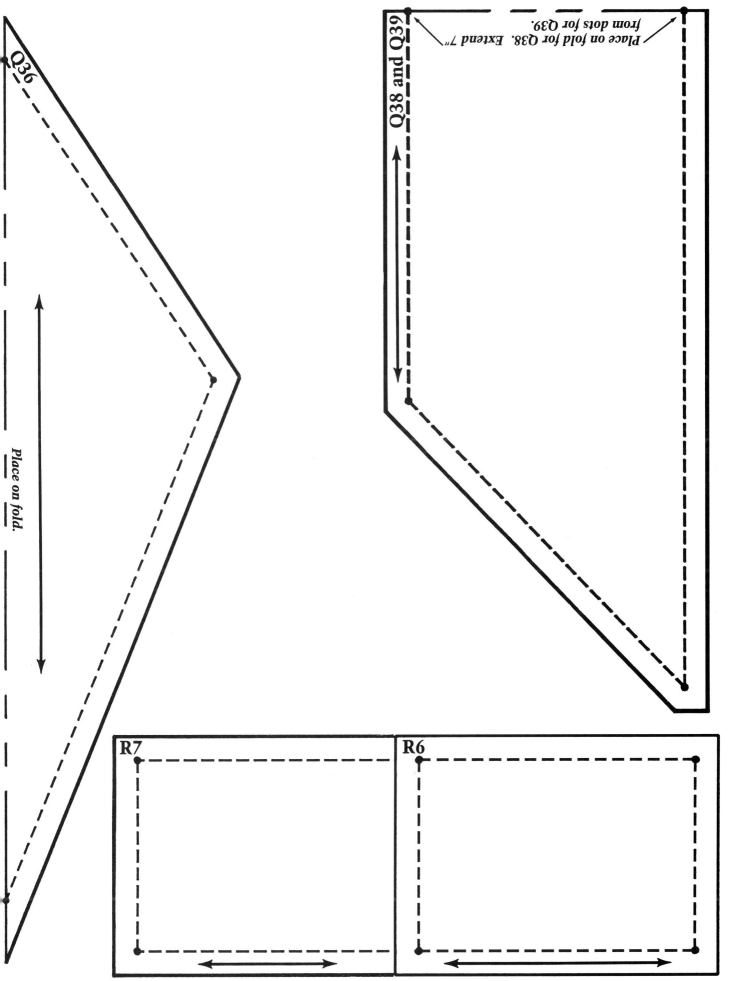

Q36

Place on fold.

Q38 and Q39

Place on fold for Q38. Extend 7″ from dots for Q39.

R7

R6

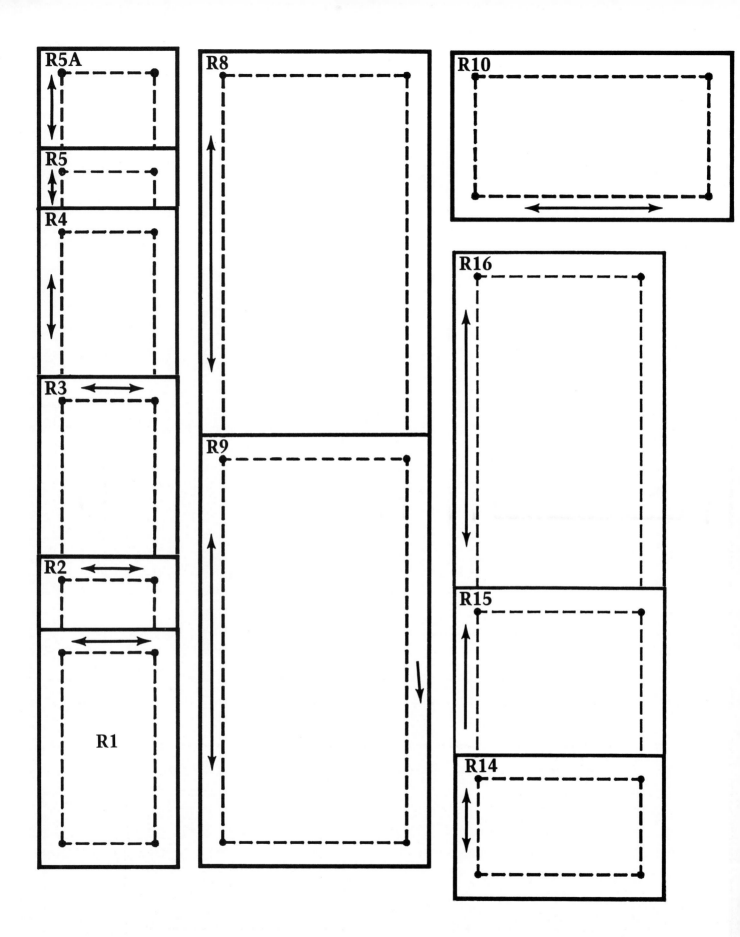

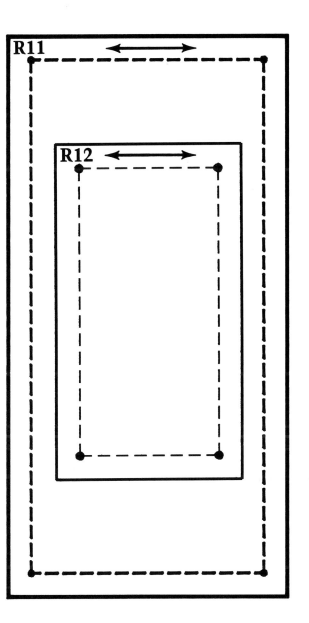

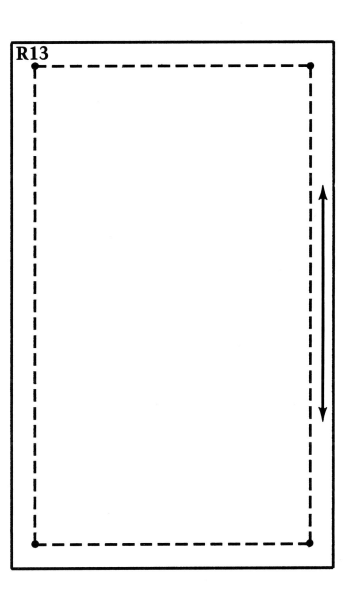

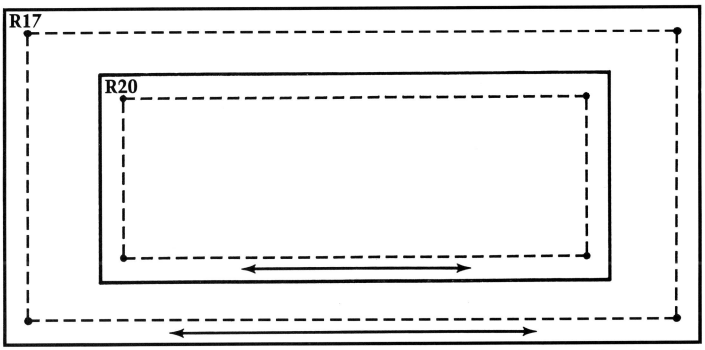

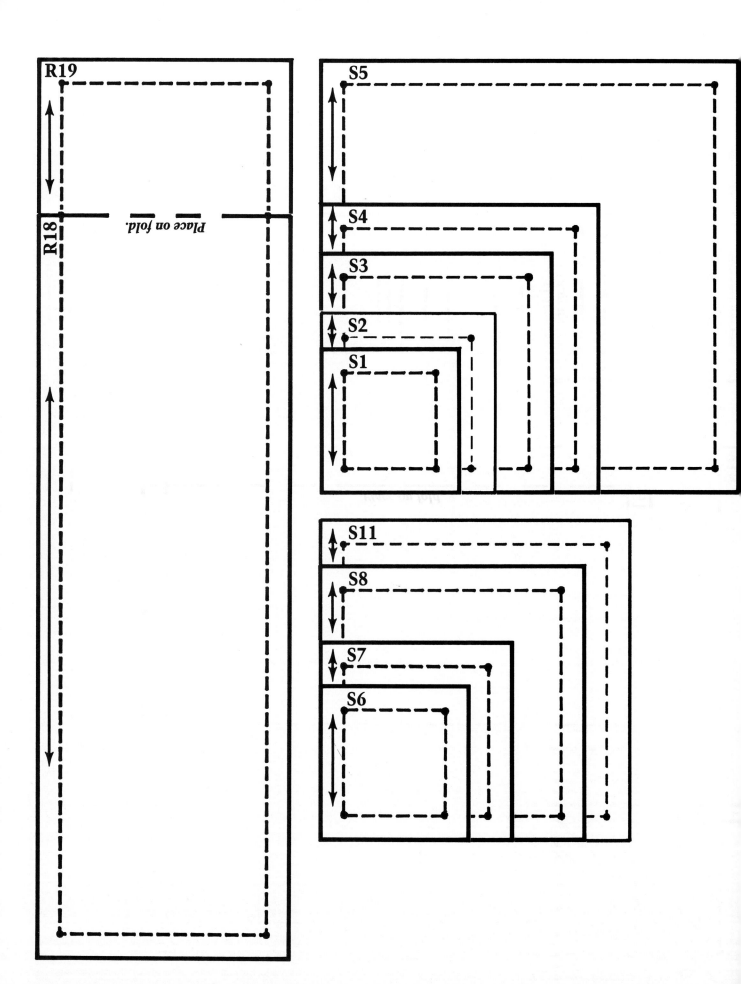

R19

R18

Place on fold.

S5

S4

S3

S2

S1

S11

S8

S7

S6

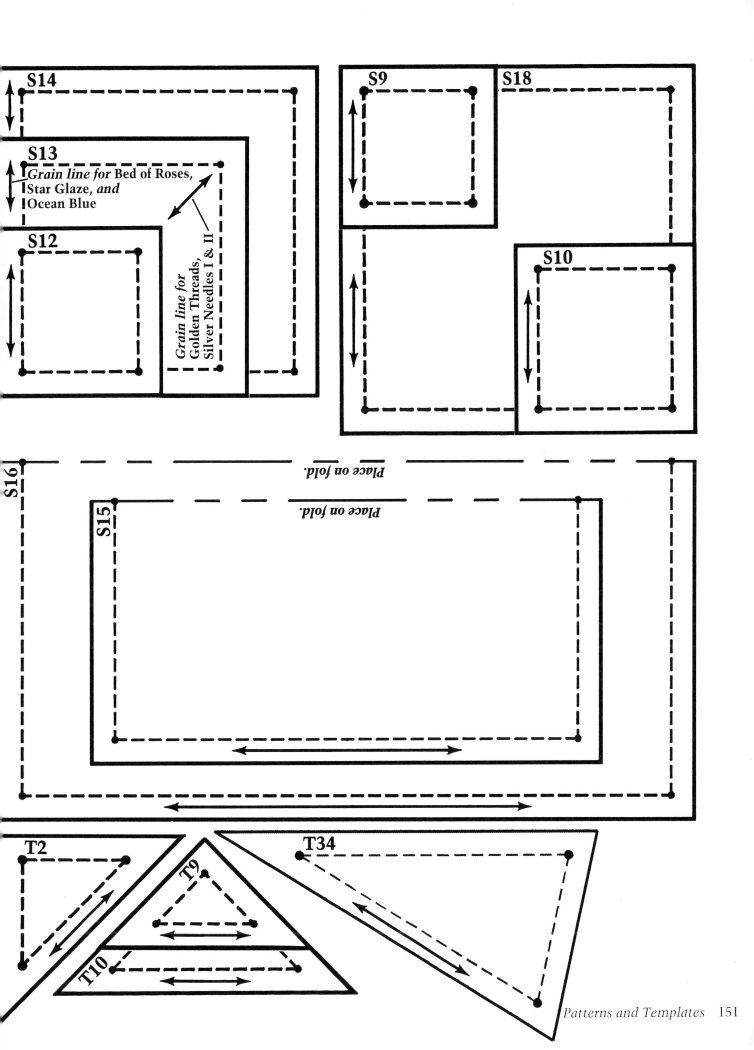

S14

S13

Grain line for Bed of Roses, Star Glaze, *and* Ocean Blue

S12

Grain line for Golden Threads, Silver Needles I & II

S9

S18

S10

S16

Place on fold.

Place on fold.

S15

T2

T9

T10

T34

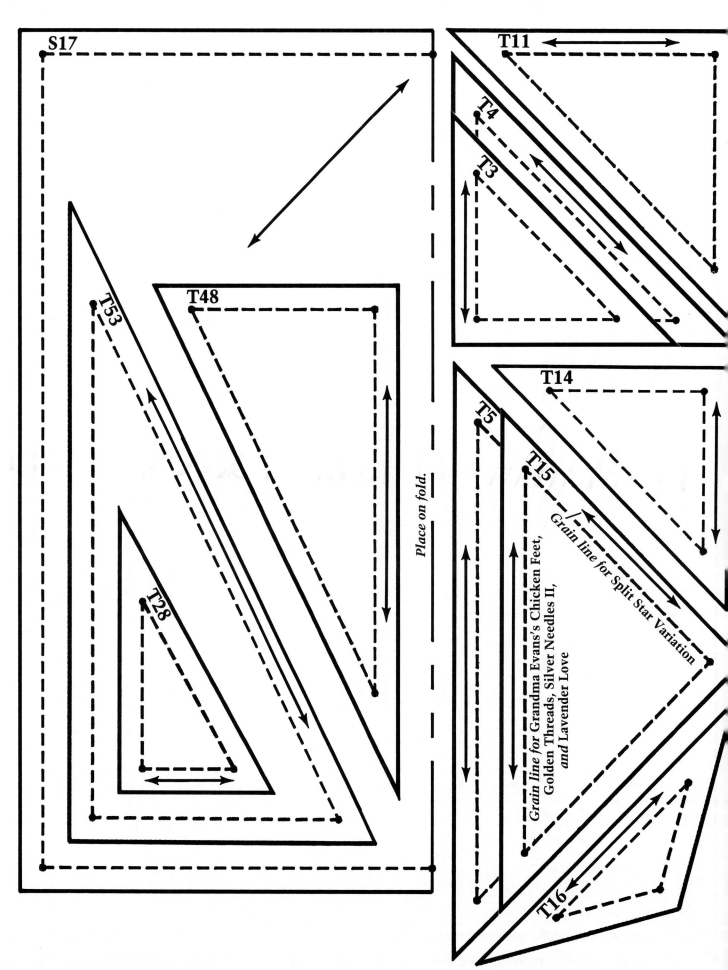

S17

T48

T53

T28

Place on fold.

T11

T4

T3

T14

T5

T15

Grain line for Split Star Variation

Grain line for Grandma Evans's Chicken Feet, Golden Threads, Silver Needles II, and Lavender Love

T16

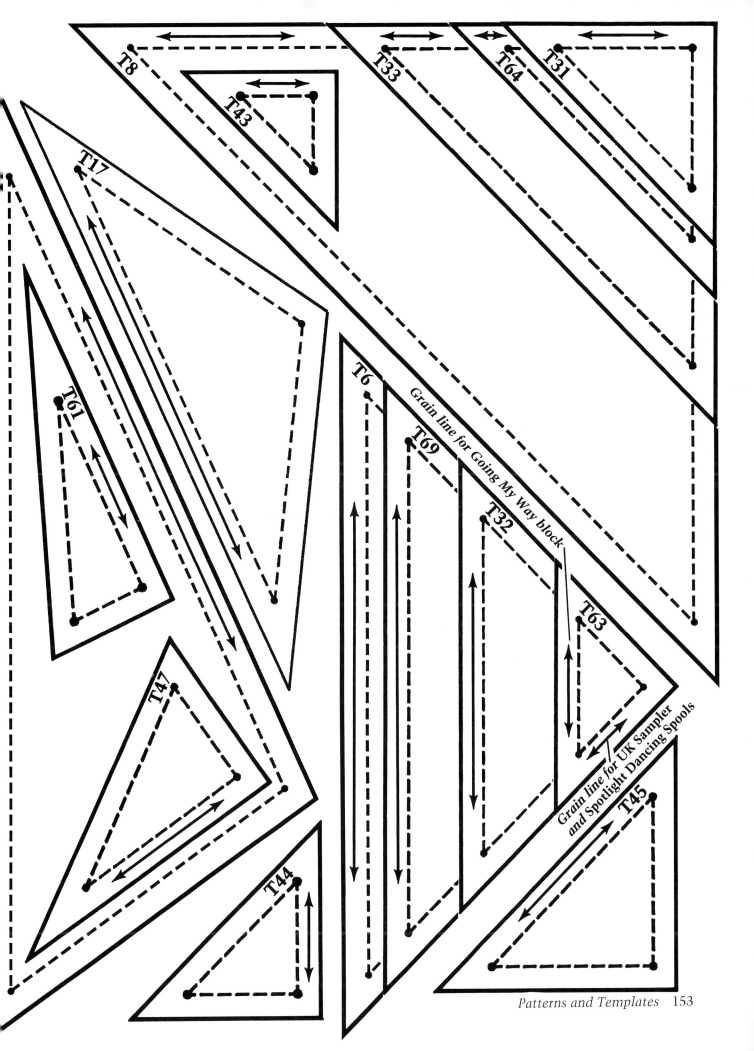

T8

T43

T33

T64

T31

T17

T61

T6

T69

Grain line for Going My Way block

T32

T63

T47

T44

Grain line for UK Sampler
and Spotlight Dancing Spools

T45

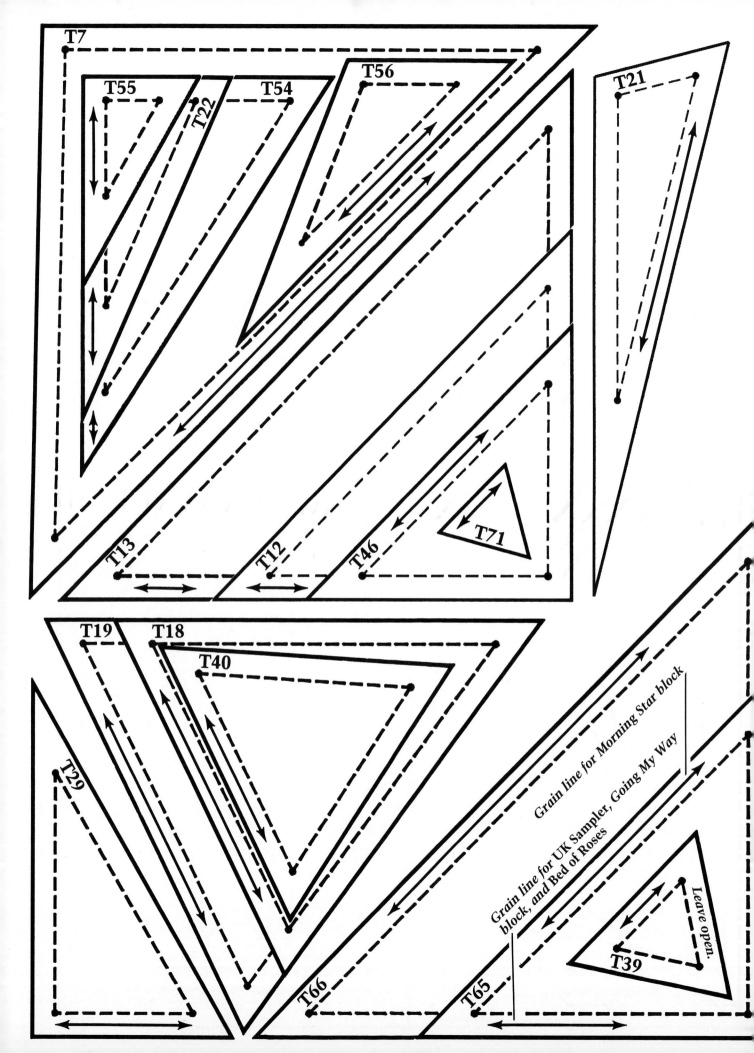

T7

T55

T54

T56

T22

T21

T13

T12

T46

T71

T19

T18

T40

T29

Grain line for Morning Star block

Grain line for UK Sampler, Going My Way block, and Bed of Roses

T66

T65

Leave open.

T39

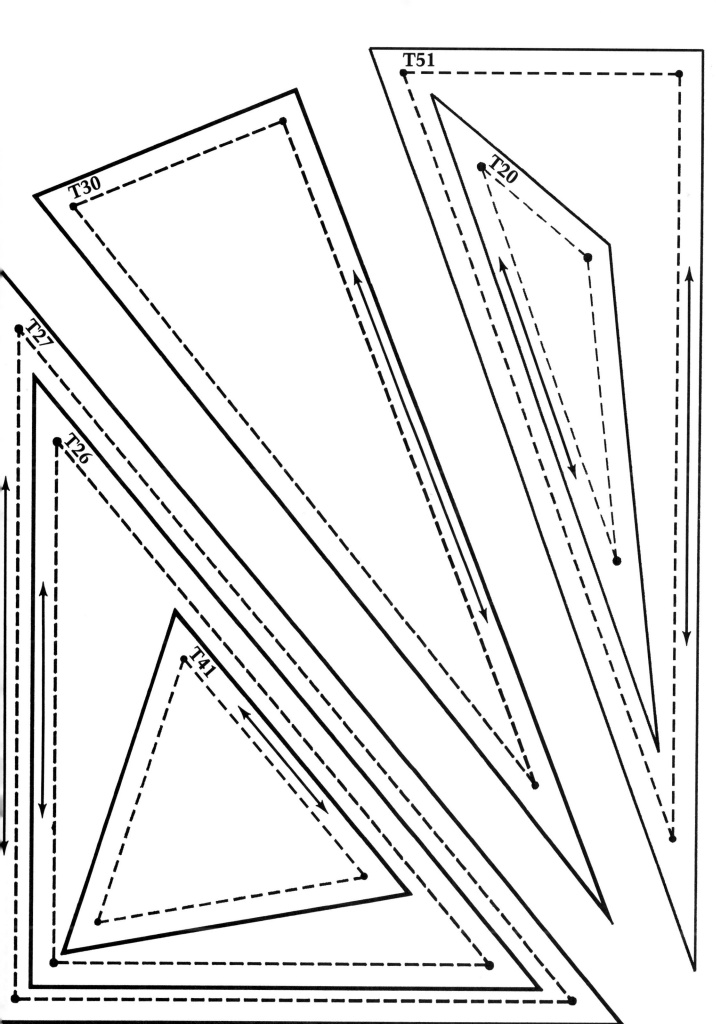

T51

T30

T20

T27

T26

T41

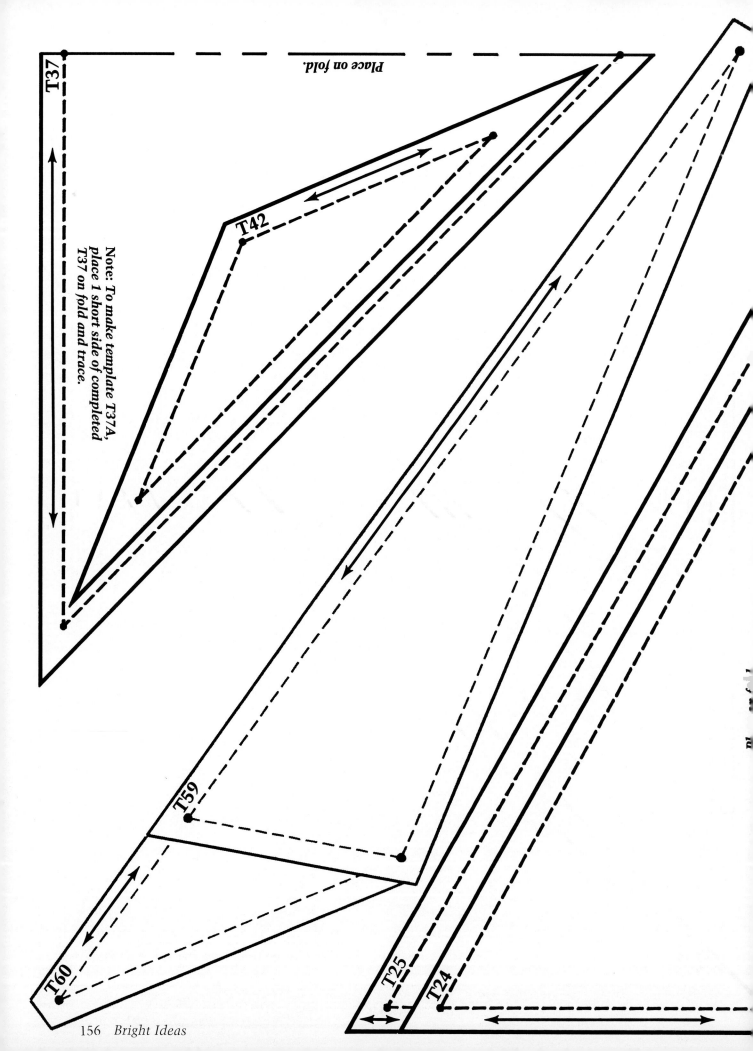

T37

Place on fold.

Note: To make template T37A,
place 1 short side of completed
T37 on fold and trace.

T42

T59

T60

T25

T24

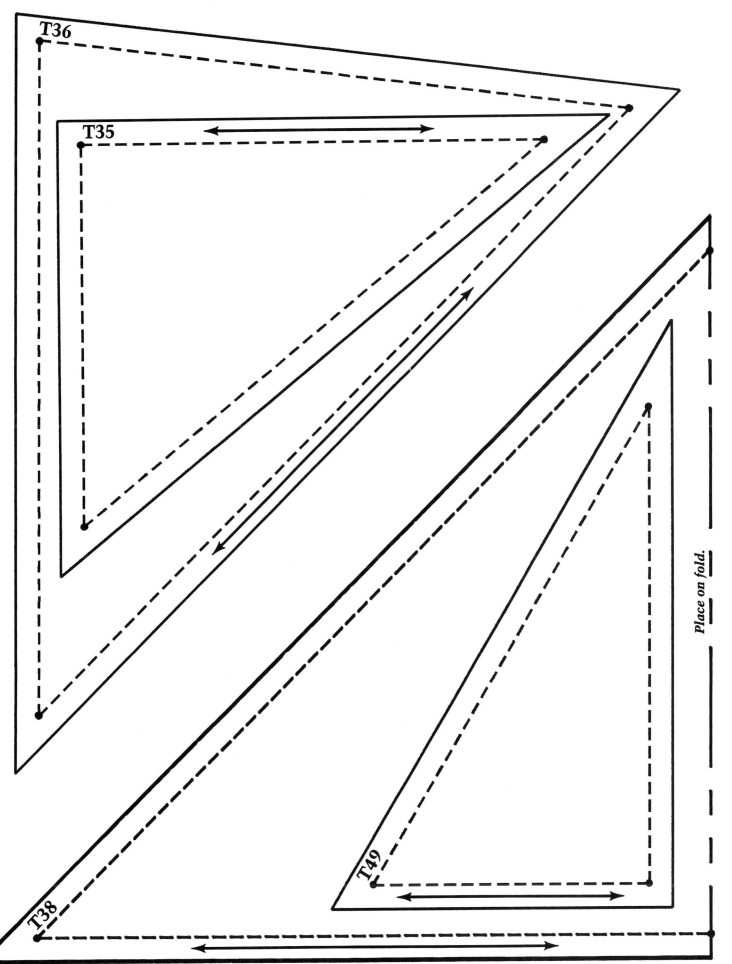

T36

T35

T38

T49

Place on fold.

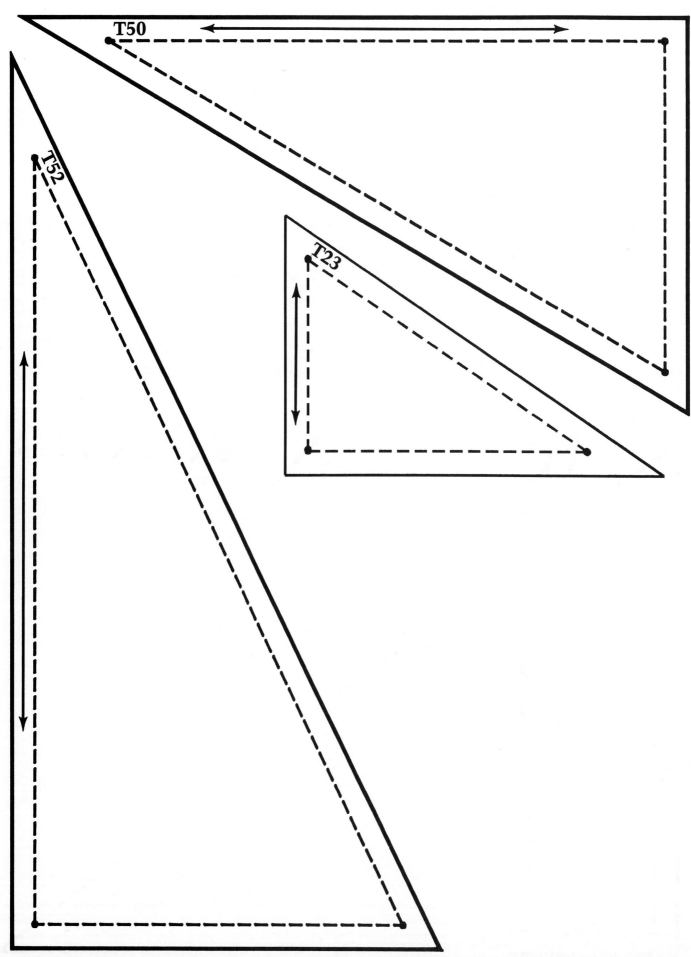

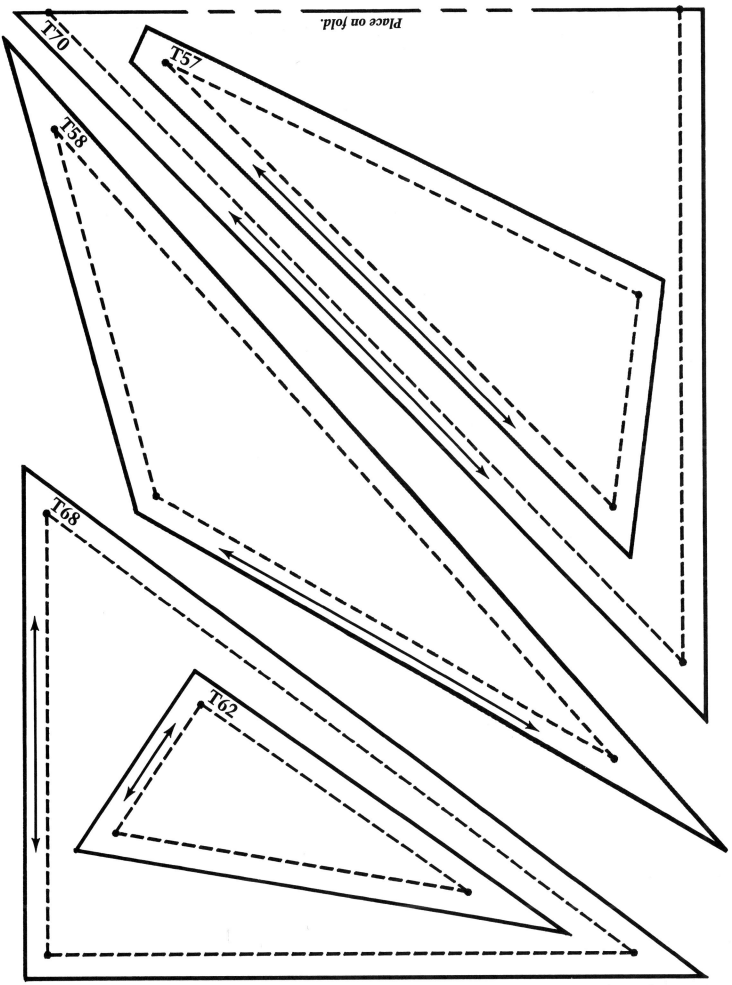

Place on fold.

T70

T57

T58

T68

T62

Place on fold.

CONTRIBUTORS

Bricktown, page 10; *Spotlight Dancing Spools*, page 19; *Plaid Pinwheels*, page 32; *Star Glaze*, page 34; *Copycat*, page 36; *Postage Stamp Pillow*, page 43; *Masks, Moose, and Qupak*, page 46; *Qupak Workshirt*, page 51; *Cruise and Quilt Banner*, page 52; *Moonbeams Over Many Ports*, page 56; *UK Sampler*, page 58; *Strawberries and Strings Vest*, page 77; *Interlock*, page 78; *Baby Buggy Boomers*, page 84; *Golden Threads, Silver Needles II*, page 92; *Car Star*, page 94; *Pastel Paisley Star*, page 96; *Split Star Variation*, page 98; *Lavender Love*, page 100; *Car Star Variation*, page 102; *Tea for Two Cozy*, page 108; *Quilting 'Round the Clock*, page 110; *Love Knot*, page 112; and *Modern Moon Over the Mountain*, page 118, designed, pieced, and quilted by Georgia Bonesteel.

Dewey Decimal 746, page 13, designed by Betsy Freeman; pieced and quilted by Landrum Library Quilters, Landrum, South Carolina.

Bed of Roses, page 16, designed, pieced, and quilted by Bloomington, Indiana, Quilters' Guild.

Autumn Windows, page 22, designed, pieced, and quilted by Alice Thomure.

Little Toot, page 24, designed, pieced, and quilted by Marilyn Fluharty.

Hillside Village, page 26, designed and pieced by Georgia Bonesteel; border pieced by Karol Roe; quilted by Linda Honsberger.

Grandma Evans's Chicken Feet, page 30, and *Singapore Stars*, page 62, designed, pieced, and quilted by Penny Wortman.

Ocean Blue, page 38, designed, pieced, and quilted by Maruszka V. Hufstader.

The Ultimate Postage Stamp Quilt, page 40, designed by Georgia Bonesteel; pieced and quilted by the Western North Carolina Quilters Guild.

The Big Ship, page 54, designed, pieced, and quilted by Georgia Bonesteel; sails by Karen Pervier, Helen Kelley, Doreen Speckman, and Virginia Avery.

Amish Images, page 66, designed and pieced by Georgia Bonesteel; quilted by Marie Detwiler and her quilting group from Princess Anne, Maryland.

Hipp Strip, page 72, designed pieced, and quilted by Georgia Bonesteel; partial piecing by Joan Pierro and Peggy Genung.

Woven Wonder, page 74, designed by Georgia Bonesteel; pieced and quilted by Judy Rankin.

Manteca Ribbons, page 81, designed by Georgia Bonesteel; pieced and quilted by Manteca Quilters Guild, Manteca, California.

Log Lanterns, page 86, designed and pieced by Karen Pervier; quilted by Wendy Crigger.

Golden Threads, Silver Needles I, page 90, designed and pieced by Georgia Bonesteel; partial piecing by Glenda Gussman and Judy Rankin; special assistant, Virginia Jinkinson; quilted by Georgia Bonesteel and Linda Honsberger.

House Exchange Program, page 106, designed, pieced, and quilted by Georgia Bonesteel, Sheila Scawen, and the Freedom Escape Quilters.

Decorator's Cover, page 114, designed, pieced, and quilted by Jill Moore.

Special thanks to the following for sharing their homes, businesses, and resources: Susan Albers; Sara Jo and Jack Blackwood; Botanical Gardens of Birmingham; Mr. and Mrs. L. C. Boyd; Cabin Fever; Mr. and Mrs. Donald Chaney, Sr.; Children's Dance Foundation; Duke University Hospital; Mr. and Mrs. J. F. Egolf; Egolf Motors, Inc.; First Federal Savings Bank of Hendersonville; Donna Green; Mr. and Mrs. Ted Hipp; Ellen Hobbs; Honeysuckle Hollow Antiques; Mary-Gray Hunter; Lorna Katz; Ruth and Ed Lamonte; Susan McMasters; Mintz Brothers Builders; Mr. and Mrs. Ty Rhodes; Richard Tubb Interiors; Rich's; Alice Schleusner; Tom Shipman; Steve and Bunny Smith; Katie Stoddard; Barbara Stone; Ralph M. Terceira; Norma Thomas; Margery and Louis Wilhite; Mike Wilson; and Robert Wilson.

Other works by Georgia Bonesteel
Books
  *Lap Quilting
    with Georgia Bonesteel*
  *More Lap Quilting
    with Georgia Bonesteel*
  New Ideas for Lap Quilting
Video
  *Lap Quilting
    with Georgia Bonesteel #1*
  Come Quilt with Georgia
  At Home with Georgia
Pattern Club
  Spinning Spools

For a free copy
of *The Lap Quilter,
Time-Tested Tools for
Today's Quilter from
Georgia Bonesteel*, send your
name, address, and a
first-class postage stamp to:
The Lap Quilter
P.O. Box 96,
Flat Rock, NC 28731.